food for cooks

Clare Ferguson

photography by David Munns

food for cooks

whitecap

To all food lovers
who know there will always be
more to discover
and to all those dear to me
for their forbearance

First published in 2003 by Jacqui Small,
an imprint of Aurum Press Ltd, 25 Bedford Avenue,
London WC1B 3AT

Published in Canada in 2003 by Whitecap Books
For more information, please contact
Whitecap Books Ltd,
351 Lynn Avenue,
North Vancouver, British Columbia,
Canada, V7J 2C4

Publisher Jacqui Small
Art Director Janet James
Food Stylist Clare Ferguson
Props Stylist Victoria Allen
Project Editor Emily Hatchwell
Recipe Editor Madeline Weston
Production Geoff Barlow

ISBN: 1 55285 533 3

Printed and bound in China

RECIPE NOTES

Spoon measurements Recipes use standard measuring spoons and cups. Measurements are level unless otherwise stated.
Ovens Recipes in this book were tested with a convection oven. If using a conventional oven, increase the temperature by 70°F, or follow the manufacturer's instructions.
Microwave ovens Where a microwave oven was used, this was at 750–900 watts on high power; if using a microwave oven that is appreciably lower or higher in wattage, timings should be adjusted accordingly.
Herbs Fresh herbs are used unless otherwise stated. If substituting dried herbs, use a half or a quarter of the amount, or substitute another fresh herb.
Oils Use the oils specified whenever possible, and avoid any vegetable oils of unidentifiable provenance.
Butter If neither salted or unsalted butter is specified, use your own preferred kind.
Eggs are large, unless specified otherwise.
Raw foods Dishes containing raw or partly cooked eggs, raw milk cheeses, raw or rare-cooked meat or fish products should not be served to very young children or to the elderly, or to anyone who is pregnant.
Serving temperature For reasons of safety, foods that are served hot or warm should be eaten within 90 minutes; if more time elapses, they should be refrigerated.

contents

introduction

Good cooking is not about luxury ingredients, it is about everyday resourcefulness, creativity, and inspiration. Curiosity helps, as does a sense of humor about the mysteries of the kitchen.

These pages and pictures are for all those cooks who long to discover more about food and cooking but don't know where to start; and for all food lovers who like vivid, interesting flavors, or who enjoy exotic or deeply traditional foods but need help in turning them into a delicious dish.

Producing real, simple meals from scratch, day by day, using decent raw materials, is an underrated skill. It sometimes seems harder to achieve as our free time shrinks and as frozen meals beckon from the supermarket display cabinets. Available time for food shopping, once one of life's more enjoyable leisure pursuits, often loses out to overdue housework or dealing with the email inbox.

True hospitality is an instinct, but spur-of-the-moment invitations to lunch or dinner may often depend on a well-stocked pantry.

What are foods for cooks?

The more than 500 ingredients chosen for inclusion in this book—some basic, some esoteric—are a personal selection. What these larder foods, drinks, flavorings and cooking aids have in common is that they have all been preserved or packaged in some way, so they can be bought in advance and stored on a shelf for days, weeks, or even months.

Once upon a time, preserved foods consisted of a small range of worthy ingredients put away for emergencies or the winter. Today, however, our cabinets and pantries are crammed with a vast range of intriguing and versatile preserved foods from all corners of the country and the world. Interestingly, in this modern era of refrigeration and globally accessible fresh foods, we eat preserved foods not so much out of necessity but simply because we enjoy the taste.

This book evaluates the potential of all these ingredients and provides hundreds of ideas for using them—combined or not with the fresh foods that we must buy on a more regular basis. Of course, it is unthinkable to live without fresh milk, bread, eggs, herbs and garlic, not to mention fresh fruit and vegetables and fresh meat and fish, but good larder ingredients will add fluency, freedom and fascination to your cooking and will also help you to produce stylish and relaxed meals. They are the secret weapon that can transform reasonable raw materials into inspirational dishes and help make cooking fun.

Authenticity of ingredients

Decent cooking is knowing how to use "common ingredients produced uncommonly well", to quote the superb Irish cook, Myrtle Allen. It is also knowing how to select the right ones for the task. The best long-life foods are those whose tastes, textures, and appearances have not been compromised. Some modifications are delicious, others are not.

An important clue as to the quality of any food, from cookies to bacon, is that, generally, you get what you pay for. You can also judge from a short, honest ingredients list—which should include few or no additives such as stabilizers, colorants, flavorings, or preservatives—whether the food is a properly prepared food or an industrial product made out of the left-overs of another manufacturing process, or simply a low-quality product.

Understanding the label

The list of ingredients states, on Tabasco sauce, for example, simply "vinegar, red pepper and salt"; on chocolate paste, "chocolate, sugar syrup, cream". (Ingredients are listed in order of the volume used.) Many foods, however, contain more complex ingredients than this, including additives such as colorings, preservatives, and stabilisers. Some of these are certainly not a welcome addition to food, but others are perfectly acceptable. Glucose syrup, vitamin C and tartaric acid—cooking aids included in this book—all fall into this category.

"Nature identical" flavors (that is, chemically identical to the natural flavor) are laboratory created but can enhance some foods if used wisely, although natural flavors are, of course, the ideal. Truffle oil, for example, may be flavored with both real truffle fragments and "nature identical" flavorings.

Another clue as to the quality of any product is whether it has a "denomination"—the defined, strictly regulated identity, based on geographical location, that distinguishes a particular (often artisanal) product from any other like it. Terms used to denote this, such as AOC (Appellation d'Origine Contrôlée) in France, and DOC (Denominazione di Origine Controllata) in Italy, can apply to cheese, butter, vinegar, and even lentils, as well as, most famously, to wines. (There is no real equivalent in the United States.) If you buy Parmesan cheese that doesn't proudly state its denomination, you are not buying a product of guaranteed quality. Someone once quipped "Never buy anything not signed", and it is not a bad maxim.

The important issues of organic or sustainable production, along with genetic modification, must be matters for personal debate: so choose for yourself.

The preservation process

Preservation, whether of artisanal or of mass-market foods, can be achieved by drying, pickling, salting, curing, smoking, or heating—that is, by changing the normal concentration of liquid within the food's cells. Air, sun, heat, acids, sugars, syrups, fats, spices, herbs, waxes, and alcohols can all be used to lengthen a food's shelf life. So can appropriate packaging.

Thanks to modern technological advancements, methods to prolong the "keepability" of foods have been revolutionized over recent decades. Foods may now come gas-packed, vacuum-packed, pasteurized, ultra-heat-treated, sterilized, semi-cooked ("mi-cuit"), kiln-dried, or freeze-dried. And pop-top, pull-tab and other inventive lids now offer tamper-proof ways to close containers and ensure freshness and safety. Not all such methods produce good results all of the time, however. You must experiment, taste and decide for yourself which foods you like.

Even when buying products with a famously long shelf life, such as legumes or grains, it is generally best to buy foods little and often. Even if lentils and rice are perfectly usable after one year, their flavor will certainly have deteriorated.

The refrigerator is an undeniably useful storage place, but many foods taste better if stored in a cool, dark but not refrigerated place, whether it is a walk-in pantry or a cupboard. Perishable foods should be kept refrigerated in the hottest months of the year.

How to buy the best

There are many ways to access the global pantry and enjoy the world's best ingredients. Get to know and appreciate the street markets, farmers' markets and farm shops, if they exist, in your area. Make an effort to explore every kind of food shop, including ethnic grocers, specialist delicatessens, wholefood shops and luxury department stores. Wherever immigrant communities thrive, you will find a rich source of interesting and unusual foodstuffs, and their shops allow you to learn about their food culture at first hand. In recent decades, supermarkets have massively changed our consumer purchasing habits, in some ways for the worse, but they have, at the same time, brought international foods to a wider audience.

Mail-order suppliers, often with the help of the Internet, have also tapped into what modern, shoppers need: individual service, good ingredients, and time-saving efficiency.

This book

Food for Cooks is not an encyclopaedia, but a user-friendly handbook that will hopefully inspire you to cook better than ever, as well as encourage a sense of adventure and discovery. In addition to the many hundreds of ideas provided in the descriptions of individual ingredients, the book includes more than 70 illustrated recipes. I have been hugely fortunate to be able to use, alongside my own recipes, selected recipe contributions from a handful of the world's most famous and talented cooks, chefs and restaurateurs. Many of these are colleagues, friends and my own food heroes. To them, for their faith in this project and their generous good wishes, I say a special thank you.

At the back of the book is a list of suppliers, which includes many sources of the ingredients featured in *Food for Cooks*.

We have had the good luck to live, for two decades, in the middle of one of London's most delectable food locations: Notting Hill. To be surrounded by extraordinarily good delis, spice merchants, ethnic grocers, traditional, rare-breed and halal butchers, bakers, *charcutiers*, *pâtissiers*, fishmongers, cheesemongers and specialist food suppliers, let alone the exuberant stall holders of Portobello Road market, is an enduring joy and a constant education.

Cheers and *bon appétit!*

Clare Ferguson

savory
flavorings

whole spices

Spices are the tawny treasures of the kitchen, capable of transforming our meals into something stupendous. They are the seeds, fruits, berries, buds, flowers, bark, roots, or rhizomes of certain plants that become intensely aromatic when dried or preserved. Their heady aroma emanates from volatile essential oils that become concentrated within the spice as it dries. Once a whole spice is crushed, the oils are released and quickly evaporate into the atmosphere, so it is usually best to buy the whole spice rather than its ground counterpart. And it is important to grind spices only when you are ready to cook. Many spices can, of course, be used in sweet dishes, but most are used more often in savory preparations.

1 Peppercorns The essential kitchen spice, peppercorns come in various guises. Black peppercorns (a) are picked as unripe berries, which are then sun-dried. The white peppercorn (b) is the same berry, only riper and with the outer layer removed. White pepper is very mild and offers heat rather than flavor. Green peppercorns (c), unripe berries from the same plant, are available brined, pickled, or dried. These work well in steak sauces, or crushed in seasoning mixes.

Pink (or red) peppercorns (d), which come from a different plant, are used for spiciness and colorfulness rather than hotness. Chinese Szechuan (or Sichuan) peppercorns (e) are fragrant, but not incendiary. Toast and then grind them, and use in rubs or in fried dishes with fish or chicken.

2 Mustard seeds Tiny perfect spheres, mustard seeds come in black, brown, and white. Black mustard seeds (a) are hard to harvest and are nowadays often replaced by brown, which are less pungent. White mustard seeds (b) are more bitter and have strong preservative powers. They are useful in vinegars, for pickling. The hot mustard oil that the seeds contain emerges only when the seeds are soaked.

storage

Buy spices little and often, use them quickly, and, above all, ditch them once they fade in taste and smell—probably after about six months. Store them, airtight, in a cool, dark, and dry place: A larder or drawer is perfect, a spice rack next to your stove is not. Use dark glass, china, or metal containers, and label them with the date of purchase.

3 Juniper berries These plump berries are sweet and pungent, and enrich game, such as venison or partridge, pork pâtés, and potato dishes. Squash the berries to a paste or lightly crush before use.

4 Cinnamon bark or sticks The intense aroma of cinnamon excels in both savory and sweet dishes. Superbly versatile, it finds a home in everything from casseroles to coffee, and in numerous spice mixes, from apple pie mix to garam masala. In Europe, it is a popular ingredient for baking, while in the Middle East it is essential in many lamb dishes.

5 Saffron The dried stigmas of the *Crocus sativus* plant are the world's costliest spice. When dried into fragile threads, saffron has an intense, musky odor that is vital in dishes such as paella, bouillabaisse, and biriani. Syrups, glazes, cakes, and icings also taste and look gorgeous with saffron added. Always use saffron in tiny amounts: too much can repel. Add it late in cooking, either soaked in a liquid or crushed (see page 16).

6 Nutmeg with mace When freshly grated, this aromatic seed has a pungent, warming taste. It is useful in both savory and sweet cooking, whether it's in cheese dishes or apple puddings. Try to buy nutmeg that still has its red, weblike outer layer, or mace, which is similar in flavor to nutmeg, but mellower.

7 Cloves The tongue-numbing flavor of these dried buds makes them ideal for pickle-making, but offensive if used in large quantities. The clove is perfect for stabbing into a peeled onion for scenting stock or bread sauce, or into the fat of a joint of ham. Cloves taste good with apple, or pound them with sugar and cinnamon to make a fruit crumble spice mix.

8 Star anise This woody seed head contains shiny red brown and highly perfumed seeds. Spicy but bitter, the crushed or whole heads or seeds enliven many Chinese dishes. For a quick aromatic fruit salad, make a sugar-based syrup (see page 44) and add a few whole heads, along with cinnamon and vanilla.

9 Fenugreek seeds These hard seeds are most useful in spice mixes, and are a vital ingredient in curry powder (see page 13). Also used in pickling, fenugreek needs gentle heat to bring out its scent.

10 Cumin seeds The cumin seed has a powerful, smoky fragrance which can easily dominate a dish. Often combined with chiles and coriander, it is vital in many spice mixes, including garam masala. Crushed, it adds savor to braised meats and baked fish.

11 Cardamom seeds These have a deliciously pungent, eucalyptus-like flavor. Normally, the green pods are simply crushed in order to remove the aromatic black seeds, and then discarded. Cardamom is common in curries, but is also good in desserts, such as apple tart and rice pudding.

12 Fennel seeds These pale seeds add a subtle aniseedy flavor to food. They are great in fish stews, breads, or herb and spice seasoning mixes. They can be substituted for dill seeds.

13 Coriander seeds Often used in Thai, Indian, and Pakistani dishes, coriander seeds give an intensely fragrant burst of woody, orange spiciness, which suits both savory and sweet foods. Teamed with chile and cumin, coriander is superb in curries. Crushed, with salt and cumin, coriander is good rubbed into poultry, pork, fish, and lamb.

14 Caraway seeds These have a warm, biting but sweet piquancy, and work wonders in rye breads, cakes, and biscuits. Pounded together with coarse sugar, caraway is good on bread and butter.

15 Vanilla pods These cured tropical pods produce a sweet and magically fragrant flavor. Good-quality vanilla pods are plump, glossy and supple, and have a strong scent. Both the pod and the fine black gummy seed paste inside can be used (see page 16) to add a sublime flavor to custards and other sweet dishes.

A pod can be reused (simply wash it and dry it), though its flavor will be weakened.

ground spices

While a spice's aroma will gradually diminish and fade (due to the spice's increased surface area) once ground, certain preground spices are useful when a fine powder is required—in cakes and savory sauces, for example—or for convenience when there's no time to grind your own. This applies particularly to spice mixes, which can be time-devouring to make; furthermore, the recipes of even the most standard mixes can vary. However, you can have fun creating your own simple mixes: Spices mixed with salt or sugar can be sprinkled on all manner of foods.

1 Turmeric The dried and ground rhizome of the turmeric plant is essential to most curries, and is also useful in pickles and marinades. Or add it to oil, butter, ghee, or stock to flavor (and color) noodles, rice, and root vegetable dishes. Never overdo it, use it raw, or substitute it for saffron.

2 Ginger Dried, ground ginger— pale, pungent, and sweet—is more versatile than its fresh parent. It is useful for baking, and also in syrups, glazes, and batters. Dust some over fish before sautéing, or rub it over pork or chicken instead of flour before cooking. Pounded together, ginger, cinnamon, peppercorns, and salt make a pungent seasoning.

3 Ground pepper Coarsely ground black pepper (pictured) is useful when making batter, dough, or pastry, or for quick rubs, while the invisibility of white pepper makes it perfect if you want spotless cheese sauces, cream-based reductions, or pastries.

4 Cinnamon Since grinding cinnamon bark to a fine powder requires serious time and effort, it is better to buy ground cinnamon for using in cakes, biscuits, and other sweet dishes. Use it in glazes, in spiced butters, or mix it with sugar and sprinkle it over peaches, muffins, or buttered toast.

5 Paprika Made from a type of hot red chile pepper, this ground spice can vary in its flavor and pungency. The best-quality paprikas are vivid red and have a soft, fruity hotness: this is one spice that you can use by the tablespoonful. Use it in meat and poultry dishes (it is essential in Hungarian goulash), in mayonnaise, and in dressings.

6 Chile powder The color, flavor and power of chile powder varies according to which type of chile is used (see pages 17–18). For the best results, grind your own from dried chiles. Substitute Tabasco sauce, cayenne pepper, or hot paprika if necessary.

7 Cayenne pepper This is made, like paprika, from a type of hot red chile pepper, but is considerably hotter. Just a pinch gives a desirable, rosy hotness to mayonnaises, dressings, vinaigrettes, bastes, and rubs for roasts and barbecued meats, as well as being useful in curries, chili con carne and spice pastes. Substitute chile powder (which is similar but usually coarser) or dried, crumbled chiles if necessary.

8 Annatto (achiote) This mildly earthy, warm, orange-red powder, made commercially by grinding fiendishly hard annatto seeds, is used, above all, to provide color: Cheeses such as Red Leicester contain annatto, and it is also used to dye kippers.

It is essential for some Mexican and Indian spice mixes. Otherwise, use it in dry rubs, in marinades, syrups, or glazes. You can even use it to color rice, pasta, or grain dishes. Annatto is also available as a paste.

mixes

1 Dukkah (du'a) An Egyptian mix of toasted spices, seeds, and nuts, dukkah is delicious as a topping or garnish. The contents can vary, but often includes sesame seeds, coriander, cumin, cinnamon, peanuts, and dried mint. Dip some torn flatbread first into good olive oil and then into dukkah: delicious.

2 Cajun spice mix This Louisiana spice mix flatters the bold, spicy tastes of New Orleans cooking. A typical Cajun mix includes black pepper, cayenne, cinnamon, cumin, thyme, oregano, dried garlic, and green filé powder (the stuff that gives gumbo its body). To make your own, see page 14.

3 Ras-el-hanout Many tagines and other meat, vegetable, and fish dishes are improved by this euphorically scented spice mix from North Africa. It may have twenty to a hundred ingredients: a typical mix includes everything from cardamom and cayenne pepper to citrus peel and dried rose buds. Use it rubbed over poultry, fish, meat, or game before cooking, or heat it in oil, butter, or ghee and mix with liquids before adding other ingredients.

4 Chinese five-spice The warm, mildly liquorice scent of this spice mix gives an unmistakably Chinese flavor. The five spices involved are: star anise, cassia (or cinnamon), Szechuan peppercorns, cloves, and fennel seeds. The mix is superb with pork—try it in a sweet, soy sauce-based glaze for roasted pork loin.

5 Zataar (zathar) This Middle Eastern mix usually contains two parts thyme (or oregano) to one part sumac (see page 26), sometimes with sesame seeds added. It is great when sprinkled on lightly oiled flatbreads and then baked, or mixed into garlicky soft cheese. In butter or oil, it tastes good drizzled over poultry or vegetables before baking or roasting.

6 Garam masala Common in northern Indian cooking, but used worldwide, garam masala's hotness and spiciness may vary, along with the ingredients: black pepper, cumin, cardamom, cinnamon, and nutmeg are normally included. Use garam masala in spicy stews and curries, lentil and bean dishes, or to sprinkle over flatbreads before baking.

7 Japanese seven-spice seasoning The seven "spices" in this tasty mix (also known as *shichimi togarashi*) are: red chile flakes, sansho (prickly ash berries or Szechuan pepper), sesame seeds, nori (seaweed) flakes, dried mandarin peel, hemp seeds, and white poppy seeds.

Available in hot, medium, and mild strengths, this spice mix can be used to season fish and seafood, chicken, noodle, and rice dishes, leafy salads, and delicately cooked vegetables. It makes a very pretty condiment for rice and noodles.

8 Curry powder A European rather than an Indian invention dating back to the colonial period, ready-mixed curry powder is despised by purists. However, it is extremely popular in Britain, France, and Scandinavia, and is surprisingly versatile, being useful in anything from a Malay fish curry to an Indian vindaloo. Use it, also, in pickles, mayonnaises, and in kedgeree.

In India, a more authentic version of curry powder is garam masala (see above).

chermoula spice paste

Makes about 1¼ cups; enough for 4 servings

This vivid Moroccan paste is delicious spread over fish, meat, or poultry before baking. Simply whiz up these ingredients in a food processor: 4 crushed garlic cloves, 2 crumbled bay leaves, 1 small bunch thyme (stems removed), 2 teaspoons mild paprika, 1 teaspoon cayenne pepper, 1 teaspoon ground cumin, 4 tablespoons chopped pickled lemon peel, a handful each of fresh cilantro and flat-leaf parsley (chopped), juice of 1 lemon, and 6 tablespoons olive oil. This quantity is plenty for 2 large fish, 4 lamb shanks, or 8 chicken legs. Store any extra in the freezer (using an ice cube tray) for 30 days.

colombo spice mix

Makes 10 tablespoons

Originally from East India, this spice mix is now used worldwide. Pan-toast, cool, and combine 1 tablespoon each of cumin seeds, coriander seeds, brown mustard seeds, black peppercorns, and coarse salt. Add 3 tablespoons coconut flakes and 2 teaspoons each of crushed chile flakes, ground turmeric, and ground ginger. Coarsely grind. Pan-toast 2 tablespoons long-grain white rice until it colors and pops. Cool, crush, and add it to the spices. Use the spice mix to coat fish or meat, then cook in coconut milk and stock, adding garlic and onion to taste. Or, sizzle the spice mix, garlic, and onion in ghee, butter, or oil, then add the remaining ingredients.

cajun spice mix

Makes about ⅓ cup; enough for 10 servings

Combine 2 teaspoons each of black peppercorns, fennel seeds, and dried oregano, sage, and thyme. Add 1 teaspoon each of coarse salt, cumin seeds, paprika, cayenne, and mustard powder. Grind everything together. At the time of use, rub the spice mix over meat, poultry or game, using 2 tablespoons for about 1 pound of food. Sauté the coated meat in butter, corn oil, or lard with 1 sliced onion and 2 cloves chopped garlic, then stew or casserole as needed. If broiling or grilling, rub the spice mix into the meat, adding pureed onion and garlic at the same time.

scented sugar

Makes about 8 tablespoons

Crush together 2 tablespoons each of caraway seeds, cardamom pods, and crumbled cinnamon sticks using a pestle and mortar; add 4 tablespoons granulated sugar. Continue to grind and pound until you achieve a good blend. This is luscious when sprinkled over sliced melon, pineapple, apples, pears, or halved bananas, wrapped in foil, then grilled. The scented sugar will keep well in an airtight jar in a cool place.

yucatecan achiote seasoning paste

Authentic Mexican, a fascinating book by Rick Bayless with Deann Groen Bayless, explores the rich, earthy flavors of that cuisine and has been a huge inspiration in the popularity of traditional Mexican cooking in the United States. This recipe shows one aspect of the use of local spices for which the food of Mexico is renowned.

Makes: ½ cup

Ingredients
1 tablespoon achiote (annatto) seeds
1 teaspoon whole black peppercorns (or scant 1½ teaspoons ground)
1 teaspoon dried oregano
4 cloves (or ⅛ teaspoon ground)
½ teaspoon cumin seeds (or ½ heaping teaspoon ground)
1 cinnamon stick (1 inch long, or 1 teaspoon ground)
1 teaspoon coriander seeds (or 1 heaping teaspoon ground)
1 scant teaspoon salt
5 cloves garlic, peeled
2 tablespoons cider vinegar
1½ teaspoons flour

Method
1. Put the achiote seeds, peppercorns, oregano, cloves, cumin, cinnamon, and coriander seeds in an electric grinder and pulverize as completely as possible; it will take a minute or more, due to the hardness of the achiote. Transfer to a small bowl and stir in the salt.
2. Finely mince the garlic, then sprinkle it with some of the spice mixture and use the back of a spoon or a flexible spreader to work it back and forth, smearing it into a smooth paste. Scrape the garlic mixture into the remaining spice powder, then stir in the vinegar and flour.
3. Scoop the paste into a small jar, cover, and let it stand for several hours (or, preferably, overnight) before using.

This is delicious rubbed all over 1-inch chunks of boneless chicken. Wrap them in moistened banana leaf strips and secure with long wooden toothpicks. Bake in an oven preheated to 400°F for 20 to 30 minutes or microwave on high for 5 to 6 minutes, or until firm and fragrant. Unwrap and eat.

using spices

Whole spices usually need treating in order to release the oils that produce their aroma: whether by grinding, pounding, or "bruising" (crushing); by pan-toasting, which enhances the flavor of small seeds, such as coriander or cumin, before grinding; or by dissolving or heating in a liquid, whether it's oil, alcohol, stock, syrup, or just water. While most whole spices are added at the start of a recipe to allow time for their flavor to flood out, ground spices can be added late in the cooking.

Grinding spices

The best way to grind by hand is to use a medium-sized ceramic pestle and mortar with an unglazed surface. For speed, it is also worth investing in an electric spice (or coffee) grinder, which should be dedicated to the purpose. If you are grinding only small amounts, adding sugar or salt provides more friction. Should you be short of equipment, a rolling pin or a hammer make decent tools for grinding and crushing.

Using a vanilla pod

Split the pod lengthwise with a sharp knife and add it to milk or cream as it heats. Let the liquid infuse for 20–30 minutes before removing the pod. For a more intense flavor, scrape out the seedy paste with the tip of a knife, scrape the paste on to sugar cubes and whisk them into already heated milk, or whichever liquid your recipe specifies; add the pod, too, if you wish, but remove it before finishing the dish.

Pan-toasting or dry-frying spices

Place the spices, such as cumin seeds, in a preheated heavy-bottom frying pan or wok, without any oil. Stir or shake continuously over medium to high heat for 1 to 3 minutes, until the seeds start to become aromatic and change color. Don't worry if they start to pop, but make sure that they don't burn. Cool, transfer to a cold surface, grind, and use as needed.

Tempering spices

In India, tempered spices (that is, sizzled in hot oil) are poured over certain dishes, just before serving. Heat several tablespoons of an appropriate oil in a heavy-bottom pan. Add the spices—such as mustard seeds, chopped fresh ginger, dried crumbled red chiles, and turmeric powder—and sauté for 5 seconds. Add lemon juice, salt, and a splash of water. Pour over plain rice, noodle, or lentils: superb.

Preparing saffron

First, lightly toast a pinch of saffron threads on a piece of aluminum foil in the oven, or in a frying pan over low heat. Crush them to a powder using a pestle and mortar or the flat side of a knife: adding coarse salt or sugar can make this easier. For easier assimilation into the dish, dissolve the threads in a few tablespoons of hot water (or rum or vodka) for a few minutes—watch the color flood out.

nine-spice rack of lamb with cucumber relish

This recipe, from *Cooking at Home with a Four-Star Chef* by Jean-Georges Vongerichten, shows the celebrated chef-restaurateur's trademark French-Asian influences. His dishes, though sophisticated, are simple and bold. He says, "You can use this spice rub with any cut of lamb (or beef, for that matter: it's great on grilled steak), but small racks (of lamb) are easy and festive. And the crispy chops are sensational set off against the cool relish."

Serves 4

Ingredients

1 teaspoon cardamom seeds
1 teaspoon sesame seeds
1 teaspoon fenugreek seeds
1 cinnamon stick (1 inch long)
1 clove
1 teaspoon cumin seeds
½ teaspoon dried chile flakes
½ nutmeg, smashed into chunks
   with the side of a cleaver
1 teaspoon ground mace
1 cucumber
Salt and freshly ground black pepper
12 to 15 mint leaves
4 pieces rack of lamb (3 ribs each)
1 teaspoon peanut or other oil

Method

1. Preheat the oven to 500°F (or your oven's highest temperature). Combine the spices in a dry skillet and toast over medium-high heat, shaking the pan frequently, until the mixture starts to smoke and becomes aromatic, about 2 minutes. Grind the spices together in a coffee or spice grinder; stop before the mixture becomes powdery—it should have the texture of coarsely ground, even cracked, black pepper. (You can store this mixture in an opaque, covered container for up to a year.)

2. Peel the cucumber, cut it in half, and scoop out the seeds. Cut into 1-inch pieces (the size is not critical), sprinkle with salt and toss together with the mint. Transfer the mixture to a food processor and blend, stopping the machine to scrape down the mixture once or twice, until finely minced but not pureed. Place in a strainer but don't press to remove all the liquid; the relish should remain moist.

3. Cut little X's in the fat of the racks of lamb; this allows it to become extra crisp. Season with salt and pepper, then sprinkle all over with the spice mixture.

4. Heat a large ovenproof frying pan over high heat for about 2 minutes. Add the oil, swirl it around the pan, and pour it out so that only a film of oil is left. Brown the lamb on the meaty side for 2 minutes, then on the bone side for 1 minute. Turn the lamb on the meaty side again and place the frying pan in the oven. Roast for 8 minutes for very rare, 10 minutes for rare, 12 minutes for medium-rare to medium. Serve the racks with a scoop of the relish on the side.

7 Pepperdew chiles in syrup Relatively newly available in a sweet syrup, often from South Africa, these mild, scarlet chiles are sweet and crunchy, and are great (if fiddly) to stuff with feta or another salty white cheese. They also work well in spicy fillings, such as for pancakes. *Delicate and mild: 1–2/10*

8 Chipotles en adobo Jalapeño chiles are known as chipotles when dried, and are widely used in Mexico. Smoke-dried rather than air-dried, they have a mellow, smoky flavor. Often sold pickled ("en adobo") or in a marinade ("en escabeche"), they can be mashed or pureed and added to marinades, dips, sauces, and bean fillings; or put into stews and casseroles. You can use the liquid to pep up anything from glazes to casseroles. *Moderately hot: 5–6/10*

9 Piquillo peppers These Spanish cone-shaped, thin-fleshed and mildly spicy-hot chiles, have a fresh, smoky-sweet flavor. Often sold canned or in jars, roasted and skinned, they are perfectly shaped for stuffing with salt cod, cheese, or potato, for example. Piquillos are also superb in salads and bakes, or just as a garnish. *Delicately hot: 2–3/10*

toasting and pureeing chiles

1 Place the whole chiles under a preheated broiler, or on foil over a flame, until the skin is blackened, and then transfer to a plastic bag. Seal and let sit for 10 minutes to allow the skin to steam itself free.

2 Remove the chiles from the bag and pinch off and discard the skin, or soak it off in a small amount of hot water. Discard the skin and mash the flesh, using a little of the liquid if necessary.

chiles

Although fresh chiles are intriguingly delicious, a supply of dried or preserved chiles can add scope and flexibility to any cook's repertoire. Chiles come in many variations, degrees of hotness, and flavors, which may be enhanced by the process of preservation, whether it's smoke-drying or pickling. Dried chiles are often hotter than the equivalent fresh ones, and, as a general rule, the smaller the chile the hotter it is. The spicy, volatile oil, called capsaicin, which causes that famous burning hotness, is found mainly in the chile's core and membranes and, to a lesser extent, in the seeds. In the descriptions below, the heat of chiles is rated from 0 to 10. Try to match chiles to the dish, since they have characteristics that suit their local cuisine, whether they are the fruity chiles of the Caribbean, or the clean, hot chiles of Kashmir.

using dried chiles

Most piquancy is achieved by crushing whole chiles before adding them, while pan-toasting the chile invigorates the flavors even more. For a milder effect, use the chiles whole, but remove them before serving, to avoid accidents. Pureed chile (see opposite) and chile flakes often penetrate a liquid more successfully than whole chiles.

1 Kashmiri This long, leathery chile is often the easiest to find. It is prized for its fresh, clean hotness, as well as for its brilliant color: Ground to a powder, it gives a gorgeous color to spice mixes, rubs, and curries. It works well in rice, lentil, and bean dishes. *Moderately hot: 6–7/10.*

2 Ancho A dried form of the ripe poblano, the most commonly used dried chile in Mexico, the ancho is mild, with a plummy, tobacco-liquorice sweetness. Use it in mole sauces, soups, marinades, and bean fillings. *Mildly hot: 3–5/10.*

3 Cascabel A small Mexican chile, the cascabel has a rich, smoky flavor. It is great crumbled directly into cooked foods, seeds and all, or into dressings and sauces. Or add whole chiles to hot liquids, such as broths, and remove them later to be cored, seeded, and pureed or mashed as a condiment. *Moderately hot: 5–7/10.*

4 Chile flakes If you don't have whole chiles to hand, chile flakes are a better substitute than chile powder. They vary in flavor and, of course, heat: One chile type or several may be used, and the seeds may or may not be removed. Red chile flakes (a) tend to be sweeter, mellower, and fruitier than green chile flakes (b). Use them directly on or in soups, salads, dressings, marinades, and spice mixes. *Mildly to fiery hot: 4–8/10.*

5 Madras These small, fiery chiles, found worldwide but used a great deal in Indian cooking, give an instant clean hotness. Use them straight, or soaked and pureed. Crumble them directly into spicy sauces, curries, and other foods, or pound them together with coarse salt, amchoor (see page 26) and dried herbs to make a condiment. *Moderately to fiery hot: 7–9/10.*

6 Choricero These fleshy Spanish or Central American chiles have a rich and smoky taste, and give chorizo sausage its depth. Use them in Hispanic, Latin American, and Caribbean dishes. Pan-toast and crumble choricero into stews or minced meat, or soak them, puree them, and add them to pork tamale fillings. *Moderately hot: 4–6/10*

dried herbs

Thanks to global trade, many herbs are now available fresh all year round, so the need to buy the dried varieties is much reduced. Moreover, soft-leaved herbs such as basil and cilantro are useless when dried. Certain robust and strong-flavored herbs dry well, however, and in some cases are even better dried than fresh. Home-dried herbs, especially wild herbs, often keep the best intensity: Hang bunches, upside down, in a sunny window or over a breezy doorway, until brittle, and then crush or crumble at the time of use. Store dried herbs airtight, and discard them after six months, or when they start to lose their pungency.

1 Lavender With its pungent, sweet scent, lavender can be delicious in herb mixes or when used to scent syrups and vinegars; lavender-infused white wine vinegar is great for dressings. Also, ground with granulated sugar to a mauve powder, it is delicious in ice cream, or on baked stone fruits.

2 Thyme Heavily fragrant, thyme comes in hundreds of varieties. Even commercially dried thyme is aromatic, giving off an earthy aroma with hints of lemon, camphor and mint. It is splendidly versatile: superb in thick soups, stocks, stews, marinades and stuffings; great with meat, poultry, and game; and perfect teamed with garlic, onion or tomatoes.

3 Curry leaves Used regularly by Pakistani and Indian cooks, curry leaves have a slightly bitter but appealing curryish, citrussy taste.

They are good in Asian stocks, soups and curries, but suit Western cooking too. The flavor of the leaves often comes out when they are tempered (see page 16). Dried leaves are vital for some spice mixes: Try grinding dried curry leaves with coriander and cumin seeds, sea salt, and pink peppercorns as a seasoning.

4 Sage A powerfully fragrant herb, sage comes in several varieties of differing intensity. It has an almost medicinal and camphorlike taste, which cuts richness and goes well with pork, duck, goose, lamb, or bacon, and also excels in stuffings, cheesy toppings, sauces, and soups.

5 Rosemary The strong woody-resinous taste of rosemary survives drying fairly well. The leaves, however, become quite hard and spiky, and should be removed from a dish before serving. Rosemary

is excellent in gravies and marinades for chicken, lamb, and other meats. It combines well with thyme and lemon.

6 Oregano This herb is essential to Greek and Italian cooking, where cooks use it with everything from pizza and pasta to grilled meats. Its biting pepperiness and penetrating flavor ripen as it cooks, so use the herb cautiously. Good-quality dried oregano lasts for ages.

7 Bay This elegant, spicy herb, with its medicinal and sweetly peppery tones, is more often used dried than fresh, and is essential in every kitchen. Bay leaves underpin French haute cuisine, being used to scent béchamel sauce, stocks, marinades, and tomato sauces. Pounded together with sugar to a powder, bay leaves scent custards and ice creams superbly.

using dried herbs

Dried herbs must be used differently from their fresh counterparts. For example, they are often best used when cooked, or else need a long soak in the cooking juices for the flavor to come out. Dry-frying dried herbs in advance can sometimes help coax out extra flavor, and they can work well in herb-spice mixes, pounded together with sugar or sea salt. One teaspoon of dried herbs is usually roughly equivalent to one tablespoon of fresh.

greek salad with herbs

This superb salad, famous in Greece, is contributed by Mediterranean food writer Rena Salaman, whose book, *Greek Food,* is a real classic. Tomato salad is the summer salad *par excellence* in Greece, almost always dressed with plain olive oil and never with vinaigrette. When white feta cheese is added, the salad is known as *horiatiki*; this is often served in tavernas.

Serves 2 to 3

Ingredients

½ pound tomatoes

1 onion, thinly sliced

1 green bell pepper, cored and thinly sliced

½ cucumber, peeled and thinly sliced

About 4 ounces Greek feta cheese, sliced (optional)

12 to 16 black olives, such as Kalamata (optional)

3 to 4 tablespoons extra-virgin olive oil

Salt and freshly ground black pepper

Dried oregano, crumbled

Method

1. Rinse the tomatoes. Cut them in half and slice them into thin wedges.

2. If you want to reduce the sharpness of the onion, soak the slices in a little salted water for 5 to 10 minutes, then take out and squeeze gently. Combine with the tomatoes, bell pepper, and cucumber.

3. Add the feta and the olives, if using. Dress the vegetables with the oil and season wtih salt, black pepper, and a sprinkle of oregano.

salts

Salt, or sodium chloride, is essential for life, and is one of the five basic tastes. It can radically alter the taste of food, bringing out the flavor of other ingredients or counteracting sweetness. It exists either as sea salt or mined salt. The former can be mass-produced artificially by the boiling and evaporation of sea water, but the best kinds are obtained by letting sea water evaporate naturally. Mined salt, found in crystalline deposits below ground (the remains of petrified prehistoric seas), is a less intriguing product than sea salt and can have a more minerally taste.

According to its provenance or processing, salt can vary in flavor, color, coarseness, and purity, as well as in "saltiness." Natural sea salts, for example, may contain traces of other minerals that can affect both the flavor and color. The costliest sea salt crystals are best used sparingly, sprinkled over a tomato salad, or served as a condiment, but most coarse salt is used for cooking. Both mined and sea salt are used to make finely ground table salt, an inferior product that has anti-caking substances added to keep it free-flowing.

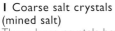

1 Coarse salt crystals (mined salt)
These large crystals have a strong, clean taste and can be used for general cooking or preserving, or to grind at the table. They may need dissolving first in some recipes, but can provide rough crunchiness on breads or pastries, and are useful for salt-baking poultry or fish. The flavor of mined salt depends on the degree of purification, but in crystal form it tends to have a stronger flavor than sea salt.

2 Maldon sea salt These highly desirable, flaky crystals, produced in Essex, England, are sea-flavored, clean, and without bitterness, and are easily crushable under the tongue, between the fingers, or with a pestle and mortar. They dissolve easily, and only a small amount is needed to give an instant hit of saltiness. While too expensive for bulk cooking, the flakes can give a delicate crunch to anything from grilled fish to soft-cooked vegetables.

3 Fleur de sel A light crystal salt from France, *fleur de sel* is the most exclusive of the naturally dried sea salts, being scooped off the surface of the crystallizing pools before the wind or rain disperses it.

4 Gros sel (sel gris) These opaque crystals from the Guérande, in Brittany, are formed naturally, but are scraped from lower down than *fleur de sel*. They may contain other minerals and trace elements, such as calcium and magnesium, which contribute to the color and delicious taste.

5 Indian black salt Also known as *kala namak*, this salt is brownish black in crystal form but turns a brownish pink when ground. It has an odd, smoky, mildly sulfury flavor. It goes well with yogurt and salads, and as part of a spicy, peppery sprinkle.

6 Fine sea salt Artificially produced sea salt, finely ground, is useful in most ways that sea salt crystals are, but is more convenient. It may lack the crunch of crystals, but it is free from the slightly bitter taste of standard table salt.

7 Celery salt Flavored with dried celery leaves or celery seeds, this salt is useful rubbed over fish or poultry, in sandwiches, breads, or muffins, or in Bloody Mary cocktails.

salt-crusted sea bass with green herb dressing

A layer of salt under and over a whole fish, which insulates as it bakes, lets the fish steam-cook gently. The resulting fish is not salty at all, just succulent.

Serves 4

Ingredients
1 small lemon, sliced (optional)
4 sprigs each of thyme, bay, and parsley
2 teaspoons black peppercorns, coarsely crushed
1 sea bass (about ½ pound), cleaned, with scales left on
About 1 pound coarse salt crystals

Method
1. Select a large ceramic baking dish or metal roasting pan in which the fish fits snugly. (The larger the dish, the more salt will be required.)
2. Put the lemon slices, if using, the herb sprigs, and peppercorns into the fish's cavity. Use long wooden toothpicks to secure the cavity closed.
3. Spread a layer of salt about ¾ inch deep over the base of the baking dish. Set the fish on top and pour another layer of salt all over it, patting the crystals down firmly so that there are no gaps; dampening the salt a little can help the process.
4. Bake in an oven preheated to 400°F for 30 to 40 minutes, or until the edges of the gills, curled and splayed outward, become visible through the salt, and you can smell a delicious, fishy aroma.
5. Take the fish to the table and invite your diners to tap and then peel away the salt crust, scales, and skin to reveal the silky flesh underneath. Serve the fish with crusty, white bread, lemon halves, and melted butter, or the green herb dressing described below.

green herb dressing

Ingredients
2 cups packed flat-leaf parsley
1 cup packed mint or tarragon sprigs
6 scallions, coarsely chopped
4 to 6 cloves garlic, crushed and peeled
2 tablespoons freshly squeezed lemon juice
8 tablespoons melted butter

Method
1. Combine the first three ingredients in a food processor and whiz for about 30 seconds, until coarsely chopped and combined.
2. Add the remaining ingredients and whiz again to make a thick sauce. Any extra, unused sauce can be refrigerated for up to 2 days. This sauce is also good with eggs, potatoes, or rice.

vinegars

A popular condiment and preservative for millennia, vinegar, with its distinctively sharp taste, is a result of the natural process of fermentation of alcohol to acetic acid. It is made all over the world, often based on the favorite local drink, whether it's wine in France, or rice wine in the Far East.

The best vinegars are those made from wine (or grape must, used to make balsamic vinegar), though not all wine vinegars are of good quality: To make above-average sherry vinegar or red wine vinegar, for example, you must start off with high-quality liquor and use the slow, traditional Orléans process of production, which results in a smoother taste and preserves the flavor of the original wine. These good-quality wine vinegars are delicious used in dressings, to deglaze the pan after cooking roast meats, or swirled into butter as a simple sauce. They are also poles apart from rapid-production wine vinegars, which are made in as little as twenty-four hours. Cheap, distinctive vinegars such as malt vinegar, produced commercially from beers and ales, are best left for pickling, or for dishes where strength is more important than flavor.

Lots of bad wine vinegars claim to be "produced in the traditional way," so it is more reliable to judge a vinegar by its cost and other information on the label: Good vinegars do not contain colorings. If you do end up with a poor vinegar, adding leftover port, sherry, or wine can soften the harshness, as can diluting it with a little water.

1 Red and white wine vinegars Traditionally, the source of many wine vinegars was the Loire region of France, but today excellent wine vinegars are made all over the world, from Spain to California.

The best wine vinegars usually specify which wine they are made from, and echo that wine's flavor. Red wine vinegar (a), made from Rioja, for example, gives an oaky and full-bodied vinegar, while a white wine vinegar made from Riesling is elegantly scented. White wine vinegar is milder than red, and is more often used for making flavored vinegars—by adding anything from chiles to seaweed;

tarragon-flavored vinegar (b) is particularly successful. (It is easy to flavor your own vinegar: Just add the herb or spice and let it infuse for a few days.)

All these vinegars are good for all culinary and table uses, whether it's in vinaigrettes, marinades, steak sauces, or fresh fruit chutneys.

2 Sherry vinegar At its best, this nutty, aromatic, and often punchy vinegar, from Jerez in Spain, has much of the character of the original sherry: vinegar made from oloroso, for example, can be superb. Sherry vinegar is great with offal and foie gras, and in gazpacho

or white or green bean salads. Deglaze the pan with some when sautéing seafood, or drizzle some into a dressing for warm potato salad.

3 Cider vinegar This mild and fruity vinegar, with relatively low acidity, is produced in cider-making communities such as Normandy, and is very popular in the United States. The flavor varies according to the type of apple used.

Cider vinegar works well with pork (deglaze the pan with it after roasting the meat), in tomato or fruit sauces, in barbecue marinades, or in simple herb vinaigrettes.

1a   1b   2   3   4

4 Red fruit vinegars Fruit vinegars can be made by fermenting the actual fruit juices, but most commonly are made by simply macerating the fruit in wine vinegar. Fruits like raspberries and blackcurrants seem to perform best. Avoid buying bottles with fruit still inside—it looks nice but can cause cloudiness.

Use red fruit vinegar with duck and other rich meats, in dressings, glazes, and fruit purees, or sprinkle it over leafy salads and fresh fruits.

5 Balsamic vinegar Identifying a good balsamic vinegar, which differs from other wine vinegars because it is made from must rather than from wine, is a minefield. At its best, balsamic vinegar is a wonderful, fragrant, sharp, rich brown syrup that is good enough to drink straight.

If you can find it, or afford it, buy aged balsamic vinegar from the Modena or Reggio provinces in Italy, which is labeled "tradizionale" and has a distinctive seal to show that it conforms to certain (high) standards. This is aged for twelve years or more and is so expensive that it is best used only as a condiment, trickled over salads or strawberries and other fruits.

Vinegar labeled "artisanale" has not been matured as long as tradizionale has, but it is often good, though with less complex flavors. It costs considerably less, and can be used more liberally, in vinaigrettes, reductions and so on.

At the bottom of the scale is the industrial-level condiment,

which is made very quickly. It may be "made traditionally," but a glance at the label is likely to show that it contains additives. If you buy this grade, boiling the vinegar down until it's reduced by half can produce a better flavor.

6 Malt vinegar This everyday brown vinegar, usually darkened with caramel, is malty but not subtle. Use it for pickling where color does not matter, or in robust, earthly dishes, spicy sauces, tomato chutney, or relishes to eat with strong cheeses. This is the traditional vinegar to sprinkle over fish and chips.

7 Distilled vinegar Concentrated by distillation, this crystal-clear, fiercely sharp malt vinegar (also known as "white" or "spirit" vinegar) is convenient when the malty taste or brown color of ordinary malt vinegar is inappropriate, and when intensity matters—for pearl onion pickles or crunchy dill pickles, for example. Distilled vinegar is a useful acidifier, in fresh mint sauce, or to mix with hot mustard, and can also be used in spicy Southeast Asian dishes. It should be used in tiny amounts, or diluted.

8 Rice vinegar Both Japan and China make vinegars fermented from rice wine. These vinegars can vary a great deal in taste and color (white, brown, and black rice are all used), but they are generally clear and light-flavored, and sweeter and less acidic than many of the vinegars made in Europe. Perhaps not surprisingly, they are well suited to rice dishes.

Japanese white rice vinegar (a) has a mild but tart, clean taste. It is essential for flavoring the rice for sushi, and gives a pleasant flavor to dressings, creamy sauces, and delicate, sweetish glazes for fish and seafood. It may come flavored, with herbs, chiles, sesame seeds, or even bonito shavings.

Chinese white rice vinegar (b) tends to be sharper than its Japanese equivalent but is also good in rice or noodle dishes, or in glazes for fish and seafood. Chinese brown rice vinegar is fruitier and fuller-flavored, and is useful for marinades or dressings. More striking, though, is China's inky black rice vinegar, which is mellow and sweet, and works well in highly caramelized, long-cooked pork or duck dishes.

storage

The high acid level in vinegar means that it keeps well, for at least six months and usually much longer. Store your bottles in a cool, dark place, particularly those containing vinegars that you use only occasionally. Since vinegar's acetic acid corrodes, never store it for any period of time in containers with metal tops; plastic, ceramic, or cork is safer.

5   6   7   8a   8b

souring agents

In addition to naturally sour fruit juices, wines, and vinegars, a range of other natural and manmade substances can help create the necessary sharp taste for certain foods and drinks, as well as act as a preservative. This group of sometimes delicious, sometimes intense substances is often neglected and should be stocked in any cook's pantry.

1 Verjuice "Green juice"—the juice of unripe sour fruit (usually grapes)—is useful when the sharpness of lemon or vinegar would be too aggressive. Use it as a dressing with greens, or to give extra depth to marinades, stocks, sauces, and even cocktails.

2 Acetic acid 33% ($C_2H_4O_2$) This acidic liquid (a concentrate of the active ingredient in vinegar) is useful for making gherkin or cucumber pickles. It must be stored in a cool, dark place (**away from children's reach**), and diluted 1:2 with water before use. Wash your hands after using it. Good drugstores should stock acetic acid.

3 Tamarind paste This sticky paste (or concentrate) is made from the pods of the tamarind tree, and is the most common souring agent in Indian and Southeast Asian cooking. With a delicious, rounded sour taste, it is great in curries, soups, and many chicken or meat dishes. It is also available as a sauce.

4 Amchoor (amchur) A sweet-sour, aromatic powder, produced in India by grinding up dried, unripe mangoes, amchoor has a lovely astringent taste accompanied by a sweetish tang. It tastes delicious added to curries, chutneys, and pickles, and works well in stews, dhals, and spice mixes.

5 Sumac This attractive powder, made from the seeds of the berrylike sumac fruit, imparts an agreeable fruity sourness to dishes. It is widely used in the Middle East, sprinkled on grilled fish, meat, or in spice mixes. Sumac balances the richness of, say, fatty lamb dishes, while also adding great color.

6 Citric acid ($C_6H_8O_7$) If no lemon or orange juice is available, crystalline citric acid, diluted with hot water, can be used to replicate the taste. Use it to intensify sourness in drinks, or to help sharpen marinades. It is available at drugstores.

7 Tartaric acid ($C_4H_6O_6$) Either powdery or crystalline, tartaric acid is the acidic ingredient in grapes and has a direct, sour astringency. It serves a similar function to citric acid, but gives a grape taste rather than a lemony one.

8 Loomi (dried limes) In the Gulf States and Iran, loomi are used to sour rice pilafs and other dishes. They are fruity and sharp, and go well with cinnamon, ginger, and cardamom, and with fresh herbs such as cilantro. Leave them whole, or crush them before adding them to a dish, and then squeeze out and add the delicious pulp before serving. Or, crush and then grind them to sprinkle over or into savory dishes.

9 Roselle (red sorrel) The fleshy, edible calyx of this plant gives a fruity, cranberry-like acidity to teas, cordials, and preserves, as well as a powerful red pigmentation—hence its use in commercial red fruit teas.

barbecued quail in a fig bath

In this fascinating recipe, the Australian food writer Maggie Beer uses verjuice, which she produces herself, to brilliant effect. Maggie explains "Steeping grilled quail in a fresh marinade is a technique I've long loved—the beauty of it is that the flavorings can be altered according to what you have to hand. Instead of dried figs, you could add grapes and roasted walnuts, or perhaps raisins that have been reconstituted in red wine vinegar and then tossed in nut-brown butter with some rosemary. A recipe is just an idea, after all."

Serves 4

Ingredients
8 quail
Extra-virgin olive oil
Freshly ground black pepper
8 tiny white or 4 larger dried figs
Verjuice
2 lemons
1 cup basil leaves

Method
1. Using kitchen shears, cut away the backbone from each quail and slip out the rib cage with your fingers. Rub each bird with a little oil, then season with pepper and allow to sit for 1 hour before grilling.
2. Meanwhile, preheat a barbecue or prepare your charcoal fire, allowing the coals to burn down to glowing embers. Soak the figs for 20 minutes in enough verjuice to cover, then drain and cut them in half (or quarters, if using larger figs).
3. Remove the zest from the lemons using a potato peeler, then juice 1 lemon. Set the zest and juice aside.
4. Grill the quail, turning them frequently, for about 8 minutes in all, depending on the heat of the fire.
5. While the quail are cooking, pour ½ cup of the oil into a shallow glass dish, then add the figs, lemon zest, and lemon juice. Finely chop the basil and add it to the fig bath with a good grinding of pepper.
6. Transfer the cooked quail to the bath and let rest, turning once or twice, for 10 minutes, then serve with a cracked wheat salad.

sauces

The global nature of our larders means that we can now use all manner of intriguing ready-made sauces to enliven dressings, stocks, soups, marinades, bastes, or dipping sauces, as well as to use as condiments in their own right. Long-keeping, often ethnic, sauces are time- and effort-saving, and pleasingly diverse. Many Asian sauces are impossible to replicate at home, and are integral to Asian dishes, but note that some may contain additives such as colorings and flavor enhancers. Once opened, most sauces (unless they are high in natural preservatives, such as salt, acid, sugar, or chiles) should be stored in a cool, dry place or else refrigerated.

1 Anchovy sauce This is available either as a sauce (or essence), or as a denser puree. Good versions are usually British or Italian, and add a flavorsome saltiness. A teaspoonful will season many creamy sauces, gravies, stocks, and clear, Asian style soups, and enhance minced beef, lamb, or pork dishes. With shredded lemon rind, lemon juice, and butter, it makes a wonderful seasoning for grills and seafood.

2 Mushroom ketchup Flavorful, intense, and almost meaty, this dense liquid is not dissimilar to soy sauce. It can be used to enhance sauces, stocks, soups, and stews (which may or may not contain mushrooms), and it works well in meat loaves, too.

3 Tomato ketchup The success of tomato ketchup is largely due to its natural sweetness, its texture, and its vivid color. Many people can't eat burgers or chips without it, but tomato ketchup is also useful for enhancing gravies or meat sauces. Combined with Worcestershire sauce, Tabasco sauce, and garlic, it makes a mean barbecue baste.

4 Mole The ingredients in this famous Mexican sauce vary widely, but the constant is the presence of chiles. Mole can be useful for pepping up marinades for meats and poultry, and, famously, can be combined with chocolate for rich Mexican dishes. You can create your own chocolate mole by simply heating a standard mole with dark chocolate, dried oregano, and broth: This is good with poultry and game.

5 Mayonnaise Homemade mayonnaise is ambrosial, but it doesn't last. Commercial mayonnaise is not a gourmet food, but it does last. Try mixing it with chopped herbs, garlic, capers, and gherkins, as a dressing; or with tarragon and tarragon vinegar, as a dressing for fish. Harissa folded through it makes a superb dip for tortilla chips. French, Belgian, and American brands are often the best for flavor.

6 Salsa de tomatillo Made from tomatillos, a member of the nightshade family that resembles a small green tomato, this chile- and garlic-enhanced salsa is essential in Mexican cooking. It is used in many tortilla-based dishes as a seasoning, spread, or dipping sauce. Use it also with barbecued fish or pork, or with salty soft white cheese in leafy salads.

asian sauces

1 Soy sauce (shoyu) This ancient Asian sauce is made from fermented soybeans, wheat and lots of salt. It is thin and obviously salty, with a varying rich and fruity sweetness. It comes either as "dark" (a), which is sweet, heavy, and rounded in flavor, or "light" (b), which is thinner, paler, and saltier. While the former is good for enriching marinades, stews, and glazes, light soy is more versatile and is superb in stir-fries and meat, poultry, and vegetable dishes. The "naturally brewed" soy sauces have the greatest depth, but account for just 1 percent of production.

A sweetened, thicker version of soy, called *kecap manis*, is made in Indonesia. Tamari is a Japanese soy sauce made without wheat and popular for use with sushi and sashimi. Also look out for sauces that are based on soy, such as teriyaki and sukiyaki, both of which are good marinades.

2 Fish sauce Known as *nam pla* in Thailand, *nuoc mam* in Vietnam, and *patis* in the Philippines, fish sauce is an essential ingredient in these countries. Made from salted shrimp or fish, its clean, fresh saltiness enhances many dishes, and not necessarily seafood ones. Try it in stir-fried chicken dishes, with shrimp noodles, as part of a tomato relish, or in a sweet-and-sour sauce. Mixed with freshly squeezed lemon or lime juice and sliced chiles, it makes a wonderful Thai dipping sauce. The Japanese version of fish sauce is called *shottsuru*.

3 Fermented black bean sauce This dark, sticky sauce can be very thick, medium-thick, crumbly, or smoothly pureed. It is made from fermented, salted soybeans and is used in Southeast Asia and China. Black bean sauce is crucial with certain classic combinations, such as beef and vegetables with black beans, and shredded chicken, pork, or duck with noodles; it is also used in crisp, deep-fried dumplings or steamed dim sum.

4 Plum sauce All sorts of variations exist, but this Asian sauce is often thin but sticky, and pinkish. Flavored with fragments of plum, garlic, and ginger, it can be used for spreading on Chinese pancakes to accompany glazed duck; added to stir-fries; or used in glazes and in sauces for cooked poultry dishes, often in combination with soy sauce.

5 Hoisin sauce This glossy, syrupy sauce is made from soy sauce and fermented black bean sauce, chiles, and star anise and other spices, and has a sweet-salt taste. It is mostly associated with Peking duck (warmed pancakes with shredded duck, cucumber, and onions), but hoisin is a versatile product. It works well in vegetable, noodle, and dumpling dishes, as well as with poultry, pork, beef, and some seafood. Try diluting it with ginger wine and/or toasted sesame oil and seeds: This makes a superb dressing for a chicken salad.

pastes

A vast and colorful array of savory pastes, sourced from Europe, Asia, Africa, and the Americas, and based on everything from cheese to olives, nuts, fish, and soybeans, can extend every discerning cook's repertoire. Furthermore, concentrated and compact as they are, pastes are perfect candidates for the pantry.

Be sure to look for the authentic, ethnic pastes: Italian versions of typically Mediterranean pastes like tomato concentrate, sun-dried tomato paste, and red pesto, are usually the best.

1 Tahini This nutritious paste, popular in Middle Eastern cooking, is made from unroasted or roasted sesame seeds ground to a dense, rich sludge. Small amounts added to sauces, dips, and dressings give a nutty taste, richness, and gloss. It is a vital ingredient in hummus, and tastes gorgeous in North African-style lamb, with olives, lemon, and pine nuts. Stand the jar in boiling water to soften the mixture, and then mix thoroughly before use.

2 Peanut butter Either crunchy or smooth, this paste of roasted peanuts is humble but convenient and very nutritious, consisting of 30 percent protein. Infinitely adaptable in cooking, it can thicken a sauce, and is a great shortcut, for making gado gado sauce, for example. Mixed with soy sauce, spices, lime juice, chiles, and stock, it makes a quick hot sauce for fish, poultry, vegetables, noodles, or rice.

3 Tomato paste Sometimes called tomato concentrate, this paste is made from sun- or kiln-dried tomatoes, flavored with minimal spices, herbs, and seasonings. A tablespoon is all you need to flavor and color a dish, the double-concentrated paste being the most effective.

4 Sun-dried tomato paste This is a relatively recent arrival in the supermarkets. You may need to hunt around for a good one: look for one with 65 percent or more tomato solids, and flavorings such as chiles, oregano, and garlic. It is useful mainly in Mediterranean-style dishes, but try it also in Asian chicken and fish dishes when a fruit-sweet taste is needed.

5 Red pesto (pesto rosso) Unlike green pesto, red pesto survives processing well. Made of tomato concentrate, olive oil, pecorino or grana cheeses, basil, garlic, and pine nuts, it is superb stirred into hot pasta or into rich meat casseroles. Try it, also, on bruschetta with a drizzle of olive oil.

6 Patum Peperium Nicknamed "Gentlemen's Relish", this salty, anchovy-based paste became a favorite British condiment in the nineteenth century. It looks unalluring but is surprisingly tasty. Try it on toasted muffins, or under grilled cheese on toast; or use it to make anchovy and lemon butter for steaks or baked fish.

7 Olive paste Thick, salty, and earthy Mediterranean olive pastes are made from either green (unripe, sharp) or black (ripe, fruitier) olives, with flavorings such as garlic and herbs added. Use them on pizzas or in pasta, or with crudités. Tapenade is similar, but contains capers, tuna, and anchovies, and is best made fresh.

8 Green pesto (pesto Genovese) This sharply pungent, fresh basil-scented paste, a speciality of Genoa, is essential for such Mediterranean dishes as minestrone, soups, and pastas, and is also excellent with fish. It should contain fresh basil, garlic, pine nuts, Parmesan or pecorino cheese, and olive oil. Avoid heat-treated versions of pesto.

9 Shrimp paste A sticky paste made from fermented shrimp underpins many Southeast Asian dishes. It must always be cooked.

With an intensely salty tang, a little shrimp paste goes a long way. Use it in sauces, soups, braising liquids, stews, stir-fries, and curries. Bean curd, soybeans, and other mild-tasting proteins benefit from its use.

10 Miso Made of fermented soybeans or cereal grains, this salty paste is vital in Japanese cooking. It is the mainstay of Japanese soups, poaching stocks, and pouring sauces, and is popular in Southeast Asia and China, too.

Many types of miso are available, varying in color, texture, fragrance, and sweetness. The most common type, rice miso, is called *komemiso* and comes in different colors: The deeper the color the more mature and salty the paste. "Red" miso (deep red to dark brown) is strong and salty, while "white" miso (yellow to brown) has a lighter flavor.

Heat miso gently, and never boil it. Use it like a stock base, in a condiment sauce, in soup, or to add richness. It is superb combined with garlic, ginger, chile, or citrus.

11 Chinese bean pastes These salty-sweet Chinese condiments, made from fermented soybeans, are similar to Japanese miso, but tend to be coarser. They can be either smooth or with some whole or fragmented beans in it (in which case the pastes may be labeled "crushed").

Yellow bean paste (a) is milder and sweeter than dark bean sauces. Use it in stir-fries, curries, vegetable dishes, pickles, stews, braised dishes, and with seafood soups. Thick black bean paste (b), popular in Malaysia and Southeast Asia, can be used in similar ways, and is also useful as a condiment in its own right.

hot sauces, pastes, and condiments

All around the globe, hot sauces and pastes are used to add color, flavor, and interest to mild-flavored foods, whether they are used as a cooking ingredient or as a table condiment. Many of the items featured on this page have a long shelf life, and need no refrigeration.

1 Smoky barbecue sauce At its best, smoky barbecue sauce is sweet, sharp, richly fruity and spicy, with an appealing smoky taste. Use it on broiled or barbecued foods, or in burgers. Diluted with water or wine, it can become a stewing medium. Beaten into butter, with mustard, it makes a good glaze.

2 Worcestershire sauce Lea & Perrin's famous sauce—thin and spicy with a fruity heat and mild acidity—is, to British people, what soy sauce is to Asians. Use it shaken over broiled or grilled foods, sausages, and roasted meats; or in cheesy foods such as Welsh rarebit. In stir-fries, stews, and sauces, it adds character and cuts sweetness.

3 Chile sauce Innumerable types of chile sauce exist, made in all parts of the globe. Some are thin, others are dense; some are chunky, others are pureed. Always look for authentic products and pair them up with food that relates to that culture. Hugely versatile, chile sauce can be used in any way imaginable,

whether added early on in cooking, later on for real heat, or as a table condiment.

4 Sweet chile sauce Sometimes called "dim sum dipping sauce," this translucent, fiery, sweet and garlicky sauce has many variations. Perfect with Hong Kong Chinese dishes, or Vietnamese and Thai foods, its stickiness makes it good in glazes and sauces. With soy sauce and citrus juice, it makes the perfect dipping sauce.

5 Chile jam This dense and sticky condiment, made of red chiles, sugar, acid of some kind, and usually garlic, is superb with Asian, Middle Eastern, and North African dishes. It works well with curries, birianis, dhals, and rice, and tastes superb with all kinds of Indian breads. A little goes a long way.

6 Tabasco sauce This classic super-hot sauce from Louisiana, instantly recognizable in its trademark bottle, contains only chiles, vinegar, and salt. The classic red Tabasco sauce

(a), is made of pequin chiles, while green Tabasco (b) is made of jalapeño chiles. Splendid either as table condiment or to cook with, Tabasco gives a lift to an amazing assortment of foods, including oysters, guacamole, blue cheese sauce, and egg fried rice.

7 Sambal oelek The Indonesian/ Malaysian word *sambal* covers a wide range of hot or spicy side dishes and condiments. Sambal oelek, the basic sambal, consists of chiles crushed up with salt and lemon juice. The most authentic versions are Indonesian.

Spicy, fruity, chewy, and intense, sambal oelek excels as a relish—serve it with satay, for example—and also as an ingredient: It peps up everything from curries and stir-fries to chutneys and pickles.

8 Horseradish sauce A good-quality horseradish sauce is great with roast beef and smoked fish, particularly salmon, eel, trout, and mackerel, as well as in some butters and dressings.

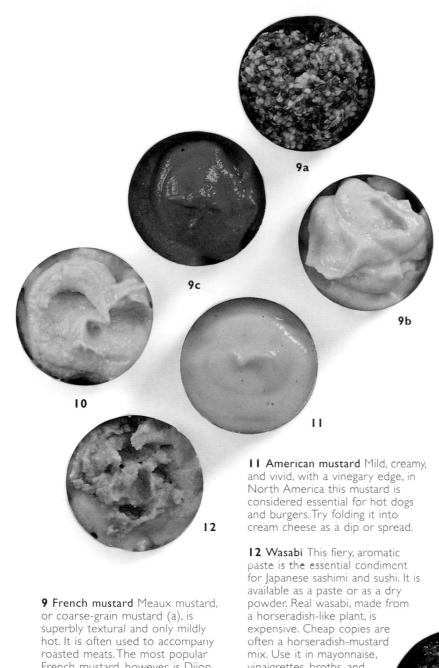

13 Caribbean jerk paste Smooth, spicy, and fiery, Caribbean jerk paste is fruity but also acidic. Use it in a marinade, or for broiling, baking, or barbecuing; or add it to beans and rice. Mixed with coconut milk, it suits quickly cooked fish and seafood dishes.

14 Curry paste Though authentic curries often need to start from dry spices, even Indian cooks use ready-made curry pastes. These can be rubbed on foods before cooking, or added later on.

There are vast numbers of these pastes on the market. Kashmiri curry paste (a) and Bombay masala, for example, are Indian pastes, while Nonya and Laksa are South-east Asian. Thai curry pastes, including massaman, Thai red, and Thai green (b), are particularly useful and usually excellent. If you have rice, canned coconut milk, and some chicken, fish, or vegetables, a Thai curry is only minutes away.

15 Harissa paste This delectable, fiery, fruity but sharp puree of chiles, garlic, and spices is a staple of North African cuisines. Tunisian-made versions are the best. Harissa is essential with couscous and many tagines, and boosts chicken and lamb stews, and vegetable and rice dishes. It can even improve pasta and dressings.

11 American mustard Mild, creamy, and vivid, with a vinegary edge, in North America this mustard is considered essential for hot dogs and burgers. Try folding it into cream cheese as a dip or spread.

12 Wasabi This fiery, aromatic paste is the essential condiment for Japanese sashimi and sushi. It is available as a paste or as a dry powder. Real wasabi, made from a horseradish-like plant, is expensive. Cheap copies are often a horseradish-mustard mix. Use it in mayonnaise, vinaigrettes, broths, and fish stews. It is also excellent with oily fish and rare-cooked beef.

9 French mustard Meaux mustard, or coarse-grain mustard (a), is superbly textural and only mildly hot. It is often used to accompany roasted meats. The most popular French mustard, however, is Dijon mustard (b). Sharp, hot, and clean-tasting, this is the mustard to eat with grilled meats, especially pork, and to use in French or other creamy sauces, and in vinaigrettes. Folded into crème fraîche, Dijon mustard is superb with smoked mackerel. Bordeaux mustard (c), sometimes known simply as "French mustard," is fruity-hot and pleasantly spicy. Milder and more earthy than Dijon, it is best used straight, with pork pies, ham, sausages, and cured meats.

10 English mustard Hotter than the French equivalent, English mustard is an essential accompaniment to British classics such as roast beef and ham. It excels in gravies, sauces, and dressings, and in cooked cheese dishes such as soufflés. Try it mixed, half and half, with apricot jam as a hot, fruity glaze for roast meats.

kebabs with satay sauce
Serves 4 as a starter

Slice 14 ounces lean, boneless chicken into about 30 thin strips. Thread the slices, accordian-style, onto 12 soaked bamboo skewers. Grind 2 teaspoons each of pan-toasted cumin and coriander seeds, ground turmeric, and desiccated coconut, to a powder. In a pan, combine the spices with 2 tablespoons each of fish sauce, sambal oelek, palm sugar, and peanut butter, adding 3 tablespoons canned unsweetened coconut milk. Simmer for 5 minutes. Let cool. Stir in ⅔ cup more coconut milk. Use half to marinate the chicken skewers for 20 minutes. Drain. Grill the kebabs for 2 to 3 minutes each side, until cooked through. Serve with the reserved satay sauce, fresh cilantro, and lime halves.

spare ribs with barbecue sauce
Serves 4 as a starter

Oven-poach 1½ pounds pork spare ribs with 2½ cups boiling water, 1 cinnamon stick, and 2 tablespoons malt vinegar in an oven preheated to 300°F for 50 minutes; discard the liquid. In a pan, combine ½ cup tomato ketchup with 2 tablespoons each of Worcestershire, fermented black bean, sweet chile, horseradish and soy sauces. Whisk in 1 teaspoon each of Chinese five-spice powder and Cajun spice mix, and 2 teaspoons toasted sesame oil. Coat the ribs with the mixture and set them on oiled foil. Bake in an oven preheated to 350°F for 25 to 35 minutes or until tender and glazed.

duck breast salad with fruity sauce
Serves 4

Season and cook 4 Barbary duck breasts halves a pre-heated griddle for 2 to 3 minutes on each side, until golden outside and rosy inside. Let them rest for a few minutes, then slice. Arrrange on cooked rice noodles, and add baby salad leaves. For the sauce, combine 2 tablespoons each of hoisin, plum, sweet chile and light soy sauces. Add 2 teaspoons dark sesame oil, 1 teaspoon garlic puree, and a squeeze of fresh orange juice. Serve spooned over the duck.

prawns with spicy mayonnaise
Serves 4

Set 3 cooked, shelled jumbo prawn tails on each of 4 serving dishes. Grind a large pinch of saffron threads together with ½ teaspoon sea salt and ¼ teaspoon cayenne using a pestle and mortar. Add 2 teaspoons Pernod or Aquavit, and stir in 2 teaspoons each of harissa, Dijon mustard and anchovy sauce. Stir this into ½ cup mayonnaise until barely blended. Divide among 4 small serving dishes, and serve with the prawn tails for dipping.

mustard chicken with colcannon

This recipe uses two mustards: a grainy type as the coating for the chicken and smooth Dijon mustard in the sauce, which helps to flavor and thicken it, and also gives color and body.

Serves 4

Ingredients

- 4 chicken breast halves (from corn-fed, free range birds), boned
- 1 tablespoon cornstarch, arrowroot, or rice flour
- 4 tablespoons grainy mustard, such as Meaux, or coarse-grain honey mustard
- 2 tablespoons extra-virgin olive oil
- 6 tablespoons Dijon mustard
- scant ½ cup dry white wine
- Salt and freshly ground black pepper
- 3 tablespoons sour cream
- Colcannon (creamy mashed potatoes with sautéed scallions and cabbage)

Method

1. Dust the chicken breasts all over with the cornstarch, shaking off any excess. Then coat them thoroughly with the grainy mustard, using a palette knife or rubber scraper.
2. Heat the oil in a large nonstick frying pan. Sauté the breasts for 2 minutes on each side. Turn them so the skin side is up.
3. Stir in the Dijon mustard and the wine, and season with salt and pepper. Cover and cook over medium heat for 8 to 10 minutes longer, until the sauce reduces and thickens.
4. Stir in the sour cream, shaking the pan, not stirring.
5. Cook until the chicken is firm and the sauce creamy, 2 to 3 minutes, adding extra water if needed.
6. Serve the chicken on the colcannon with the sauce poured over.

alcohols for savory flavorings

The appropriate alcohol can transform a dish from reasonable to knockout, and may even be essential to the dish. What would boeuf bourguignon be without a robust red wine? Some alcohols can "cook" protein by their intensity; some add an herby, fragrant appeal to stocks and sauces; others, when reduced, can create a wonderfully rich sauce or glaze. There are few rules to follow when cooking with alcohol, except always choose a bottle that is fit enough to drink.

1 White wine Characterful, medium-dry, full-bodied white wines perform best in cooking. Sauvignons Blancs and floral Gewürztztraminers and Rieslings are particularly useful. Aligoté wines are crisply dry but are superb in many fish and white-meat dishes, while oaky Chardonnay must be treated with caution since it can take over the dish. Honeyed Sauternes is superb added late in cooking.

2 Red wine Youngish, full-flavored red wines are best for cooking, and generally need reducing by half. Beaujolais, Rioja, and Grenache are all good with red meats. Pinot Noir, with a raspberry taste, plummy Merlot, and peppery Shiraz are all great to cook with, too. A leg of lamb poached in Pinot Noir, which is then reduced with garlic, shallots, and herbs, is fantastic.

3 Vermouth A fortified, wine-based apéritif, with a distinctive, herby aroma, vermouth marries well with foods. It can be used instead of wine, and has the advantage of lasting longer.
  White, dry vermouth (often French) works best. Try it in soups, stocks, dressings, and marinades,

to deglaze a roasting pan, or for poaching fish. Use red, sweet vermouth (often Italian) in red meat glazes and pasta sauces.

4 Sherry True sherry, a fortified wine, comes from Andalusia, in Spain, and can vary hugely in color and sweetness. The best sherries for savory cooking are dry and pale, such as fino or manzanilla. These sherries can transform a kidney or liver dish, and work wonders in pan gravies and in sautés of pork, veal, or chicken. Sherry deteriorates fast, so keep it in the fridge and use it as quickly as possible.

5 Bison grass vodka Clean and potent, vodka is usually distilled from grains. Flavors have been added for generations, and bison grass gives a particularly elegant taste, with a scent of vanilla. It is superb in dishes made with smoked oily fish (such as herring, salmon, sea trout, or sturgeon).

6 Scotch whisky Whisky is made worldwide, but the best is still Scottish. For cooking, use a good blend (of malt and grain whiskies) rather than your best single malt. Whisky is excellent in game and

some beef dishes. Deglaze a roasting pan with whisky and stock or wine, swirl in some butter, and season with black pepper: simple but delicious.

7 Schnapps This is a general term that describes a range of strong northern European spirits, which are usually colorless, distilled from potatoes or grains, and flavored with spices and citrus. Scandinavian aquavit, or akvavit, is among the best known. Use it in warm herring salad, flambéed with crayfish, or in gravlax.

8 Rice wine This is a very popular kitchen ingredient in China and Japan. To marinate fish, season sushi, and dress chicken and vegetables, these are the alcohols to choose. Chinese *shaohsing*, made from fermented glutinous rice, is added late in cooking and gives elegant, yeasty depth to drunken chicken, stir-fried duck, and some soups. Japanese sake is flowery, clean-scented, and delicately pale. Rice wines have a vaguely sherrylike flavor, and dry sherry (fino) is often substituted. Mirin, essentially a sweetened sake, is used only in cooking, often mixed with soy sauce.

stocks and stock bases

Ready-made stocks or bouillons are pantry basics that can save hours of time. A vast array is now available, with new types and flavors arriving on the market constantly. They all serve a similar purpose—to enrich sauces, gravies, soups, stews, stir-fries, and rice dishes—but the form can dictate how you use them, and the effect can vary. Liquid stock, for example, produces a better glaze than a bouillon cube does. Inevitably, the less-processed products, such as jellied stock, have the better flavor, but also a shorter shelf life. Choose those with as few additives as possible. Store-bought stocks are often salty, so don't salt food until the end of the cooking time.

1 Concentrate Strong and sweet-salty, good-quality concentrated liquid stocks are positively tasty. They can be added directly into boiling liquid, or used neat in tiny amounts: Try adding a dash to risottos or mushroom recipes. A good beef concentrate could even help create a steak sauce: Simply add butter and wine.

2 Fresh stock Good fresh stock should be semi-jellied, flavorful, and true to its main ingredient. Fresh fish stock, boiled down with some good white wine and butter, can become a delicious sauce. Unopened, a tub of fresh stock should last for up to 1 week.

3 Jelly Jellied stock is perfect for spooning straight into food. Look for *glace de viande* (a), a gelatinized, reduced meat stock (usually beef or veal), which can be delicious. As much a glaze as a stock, it can be brushed over a roast to go in the oven. Added to vegetable cooking water with a knob of butter, it can make an instant gravy.

Some jellied stocks come as a pastelike concentrate (b), which can give an intense meaty richness to quickly cooked meat dishes.

4 Powder and granules Stock powders and granules dissolve quickly and can be added directly to boiling water to create a stock, or sprinkled straight into the cooking pot. Japanese dashi soup stock (a) can be used in miso soup and other speedy Asian seafood dishes, while a good vegetable bouillon powder (b) adds extra flavor to rice, grain, and vegetable dishes.

5 Consommé Store-bought consommés, often sold in cans, are useful because the equivalent meat broth takes ages to create at home. Good-quality consommés work well in French onion soup, or as part of a game stew.

6 Cubes Best crumbled into a boiling liquid to be used as a cooking medium, or sprinkled dry into stuffings or toppings, bouillon cubes are generally useful rather than outstanding. But there are some exceptions. Tom yam stock cubes, for example, are intensely salty, citrussy and chile-hot, and helpful in many Southeast Asian dishes; and shiitake stock cubes give a fresh mushroomy background taste and are superb in stir-fries and rice or noodle dishes.

balsamic sabayon with salmon sashimi

Serves 4

In a small saucepan, boil 4 tablespoons Marsala and 2 tablespoons balsamic vinegar until reduced to barely 2 tablespoons, then let cool. In a small bowl over simmering water, whisk 2 egg yolks, 3 tablespoons superfine sugar, and 4 dashes distilled vinegar to a froth using an electric whisk. Trickle in most of the Marsala reduction; whisk for 2 minutes more. Spoon the frothy sabayon over 4 servings of about 2 ounces each cubed, raw, sashimi-grade salmon. Dot with the remaining Marsala reduction, add red onion slices and serve.

red wine-glazed chicken breasts

Serves 4

Over medium heat, boil a scant ½ cup robust red wine, 1 tablespoon *glace de viande*, 1 tablespoon raspberry vinegar, 2 tablespoons raspberry jelly, and 1 tablespoon salted butter until reduced to a sticky glaze. Sauté 4 chicken breast halves in oil or butter and add them to the glaze, turning to coat. Slice the chicken and spoon the glaze over, then scatter with 1 teaspoon of pink peppercorns, if desired, and serve with a pile of baby leaf salad.

jellied beef consommé with sherry

Serves 4

Freeze 1 unopened can (14 fluid ounces) good-quality beef consommé for 3 to 4 hours until semi-jellied. Finely dice a 3-inch chunk peeled cucumber, and divide among 4 soup cups. Whisk 4 tablespoons fino sherry into the consommé, using a fork. Pour the consommé mixture into the cups and top with 1 tablespoon sour cream, 1 teaspoon trout or salmon roe, and dill sprigs. Serve immediately.

vodka shooters with oysters

Serves 4

In a large cocktail shaker with ice, shake together 1¼ cups tomato juice, the juice of 1 lemon, and 4 dashes each of Tabasco, Worcestershire, and tamarind sauces. Add ½ teaspoon each of horseradish sauce, celery salt, Cajun spice mix, and sherry vinegar. Shake again and pour into 4 chilled shot glasses. Carefully, over a teaspoon, pour 2 tablespoons ice-cold vodka into each and garnish with celery sticks. Set 1 raw, live oyster next to each glass. Gulp the oyster, then sip the vodka shooter.

sweet
flavorings

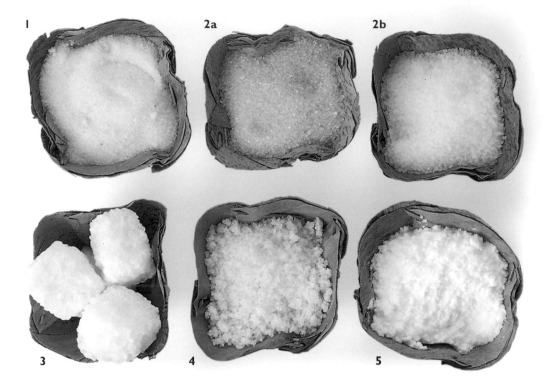

sugar

Sugar, prized for its sweetness, is a symbol of ripeness. It can be produced from all sorts of trees and plants, often in the form of syrups (see pages 42–43), but crystal sugar is its most useful form. The greatest variety of sugars come from sugarcane, produced by varying degrees of refining. The cruder, less refined states taste most distinctive, while highly refined white sugar tastes just sweet. (Most refined white sugar comes from sugar beet and is chemically identical to refined cane sugar.)

1 Superfine sugar (caster sugar) With its fine grains, superfine sugar incorporates more air than other sugars, which makes it perfect for creating lightness in cake mixtures, crisp cookies, and frothy desserts. It is good in clear syrups and glazes, and can be ground up with spices such as cinnamon, cloves, and coriander as a sweet, spicy sprinkle.

Superfine sugar is used to make vanilla sugar, the best versions of which are flavored with real vanilla seeds. This is excellent sprinkled over raw fruits and yogurts, it scents syrups and cakes beautifully, and it can improve cookies, glazes, and chocolate desserts.

2 Granulated sugar This medium-grained, free-flowing sugar is the workhorse of the kitchen and comes either as golden (a) or white (b). It is the most valuable type of sugar for everyday use and the most versatile. It can be used in both raw and cooked dishes, including cakes.

3 Sugar cubes or lumps Made of granulated sugar molded into shapes, then oven-dried, sugar cubes (which may be neatly square or more roughly shaped) are good in situations where ingredients need to be crushed—with mint leaves for mint sauce, for example—or as part of a sugar-spice sprinkle for an apple pie topping.

4 Jam sugar The coarse crystals of jam sugar contain added pectin and citric acid, which help to set jams and jellies. The crystals dissolve slowly and evenly, avoiding the risks

of caramelizing or burning on the base of the pan. Often, less boiling time is required, which helps to preserve the fruit flavors.

5 Confectioners' sugar (icing or powdered sugar) Sweet, and brilliant white, icing sugar gives prettiness to cakes, cookies, soft fruits, and pastries when sprinkled over. It dissolves instantly so it is used for mixtures, such as icings, glazes, marzipans, and chocolate truffles. Royal icing sugar has powdered egg white added, which helps pliability, for decorating cakes.

understanding the label

Due to the liberal use of words such as *unrefined* and *raw*, it can be hard to decipher the labeling on many sugars. In reality, virtually all sugars are refined to some degree, but the less refined sugars retain more natural molasses than their bleached white counterparts. The former include the big-selling golden caster and granulated sugars, at one end of the spectrum, and the brown sugars at the other. Many commercial brown sugars, particularly those labeled as "soft light brown" or "soft dark brown," however, are made by coating refined sugar with caramel or molasses. The list of ingredients should make clear whether you are dealing with the real thing. Genuine brown sugars, such as muscovado and molasses sugar, are less widely available but far superior.

6 Muscovado sugar Relatively unrefined and rich in natural molasses, muscovado sugar is dark, moist, and intensely fragrant. It is either light or dark, depending on the molasses content, and has oodles more flavor than ordinary soft brown sugar. It works well in sprinkle toppings, gingerbread, and fruit cakes (it gives good-keeping quality to cakes), in pickles, and in fresh Asian relishes.

Barbados sugar, which is similar, has a butterscotch sweetness and is good in chocolate and Christmas cakes, and in Caribbean dishes.

7 Demerara Named after the area in British Guyana where it was first produced, demerara sugar is mellow-flavored but hard and crunchy. Use it when a gritty, grainy texture is wanted: to top a muffin, or in a sprinkled crumb topping, for example. It is good in gingerbread and also in savory dishes: Use some pounded together with sea salt, lemon zest, and lime leaves to rub over fish before baking or barbecuing. (Always check the label when buying demerara sugar; avoid those that are produced artificially, by coating regular sugar with caramel or molasses.)

8 Molasses sugar A minimally refined, raw sugar, molasses sugar is fine, dark, and crumbly and has a treacly, rich, spicy flavor. Use it as you would muscovado, but also in spicy syrups, glazes, savory preserves, or savory-sweet spice mixes. It goes well with citrus flavors, cocoa, and chocolate.

9 Palm sugar This crude, dense sugar, made from crystallized palm sap, can come from a variety of different palms and is used in much savory cooking in Asia, Latin America, and the Caribbean. It is often found in Indian shops, under the name jaggery. Palm sugar has an aromatic, fudgy-sweet freshness and works well in recipes with coconut, chiles, lemongrass, ginger, garlic, fish sauce, and spices.

10 Rock crystal sugar These hard, golden, and shiny crystals (also known as rock sugar, or yellow lump sugar), are considered by many Chinese cooks to be sugar in its most desirable form. Ground to a gritty powder, or dissolved in hot liquid, rock crystal sugar can be used in desserts, glazes, or for sweetening stews or sweetmeats.

11 Dehydrated sugarcane juice A soft, intense, fudgelike sugar, this part-refined sugar suits Caribbean, Asian, and Southeast Asian recipes. In savory and sweet dishes, it adds density, color, and viscosity, whether used straight or crushed, grated, chopped, or crumbled, in a syrup or as part of a sauce.

12 Sugar swizzle sticks These decorative sugar-tipped stirring sticks are often used to sweeten coffee or tea. Made from glassy crystal sugar, which is intensely sweet and slow to dissolve, they can be used to muddle fresh rosemary, verbena, or other herbs in boiling water for a refreshing hot drink.

storage

Moist brown sugars, such as muscovado, clump and go hard if exposed to dry air. Store them airtight, and resoften by covering the sugar, in a bowl, with a damp cloth. Superfine sugar that has caked hard can be simply crushed using a rolling pin.

syrups

Essential in the kitchen for adding sweetness, gloss, and texture to both sweet and savory dishes, syrups have many different sources. Some syrups occur naturally, such as honeycomb, while others are made by gathering, boiling, and concentrating the sap from plants and trees, such as bamboo or palm trees, or by heat-treating starches, such as maize. Most significant, however, are the syrups made from sugarcane—the crude residues from the sugar-boiling process that are known, generically, as treacle. Even golden syrup, the most refined of these, contains "impurities," which are what give these syrups color and taste.

There are also many fruit syrups, honeys and flower-scented syrups on the market, which can be fun to experiment with. They include pomegranate and other fruit syrups, popular in the Middle East, which are made by boiling down fruit to create sweet-sour molasses. And don't neglect the syrups that come with canned or bottled fruits (see page 62), which are often well worth using.

1 Honeycomb This fascinating product is honey in its own natural package of beeswax cells. It is delicious crushed on hot buttered sourdough toast, or crush it over Greek yogurt or soft ricotta cheese for a quick dessert (discarding the wax after chewing if you prefer, though the wax is harmless).

2 Corn syrup Available either light (pictured) or rich dark brown (with molasses added), this heavy syrup is made from maize starch; similar versions are now also made from wheat starch.

Extremely sweet, and sometimes vanilla-scented, it is useful for keeping creamed mixtures emulsified and stable. It keeps butter icings creamy, and is useful in some toffees, ice creams, icings, and rich, damp cake mixtures. It is invaluable in pecan pie, and useful, too, in mixtures used as glazes for roasts.

3 Pomegranate molasses When fresh pomegranate juice is reduced down to a thick, dark syrup, it is beautifully sweet-sour, and useful for both seasoning and in sweet and savory cooking. Popular above all in Iran, it is also used in other Middle Eastern cuisines, but has arrived only relatively recently in Western supermarkets.

Chicken, pheasant, or duck cooked in pomegranate molasses,

with walnuts, is a famous Iranian dish known as *fesenjan*. You can also use the syrup to deglaze the pan when cooking steaks or sausages, or to rub over roasted joints. Use it in glazes, or diluted as cooking stock for pork or game.

Don't confuse pomegranate molasses with sweet pomegranate syrup, which is pink and cloying.

4 Malt extract This dense, syrupy extract, made from malted grain, is used mainly in beer- and whisky-making, but it is a pity not to use it in home cooking. It can part-replace golden syrup, maple syrup, or molasses to create a more subtle taste. Try it in whole wheat loaves, flapjacks, or baked and steamed puddings. It is also lovely spooned over thick cream, yogurt, fromage frais, or porridge.

5 Blackstrap molasses The crudest form of molasses, from which virtually all the sugar has been extracted, blackstrap molasses has an almost acrid bitterness but a perceptible sweetness as well; it is also high in minerals. Use molasses to enrich and darken cookies, fruit cakes, and steamed puddings.

6 Black treacle A sweeter version of blackstrap molasses, black treacle still has a sharp, almost bitter, accent and a tarry depth of flavor. It is useful in dark, dense, baked mixtures, such as gingerbread, and can also add depth and complexity to plum pudding, treacle toffees, and fruit cakes.

7 Maple syrup The boiled-down sap of certain kinds of maple tree native to Canada and the United States, maple syrup is wonderful poured neat over pancakes and blini, and it makes a delicious sweetener for cakes, cookies, fruit puddings, and ice cream. Or try mixing it with mustard and vinegar as a glaze for ham or carrots.

Beware of the "maple-flavored" counterfeits—a maple leaf on the label guarantees authenticity.

8 Honey This age-old food, made by bees from flower nectar, is sweeter than sugar. Single-flower honeys are generally the best (and most expensive), but cheaper honeys from mixed flowers can be good, especially if flavored with wildflowers. As a general rule, the darker the color of the honey, the stronger the flavor.

Set honey (a) is produced either naturally, through crystallization, or artificially, through heating. Naturally set white clover honey from New Zealand is intensely flavorful and excellent for general use. Mix it with butter, orange juice and zest, and bitter chocolate as a frosting for cakes, or combine it with cream and cinnamon as a sauce for ice cream or baked fruits. A good, aromatic clear honey (b), such as lavender honey from Provence, is very floral and tastes delicious drizzled over cream-topped fruits; it can also be used as a glaze.

9 Fruit syrup The best fruit syrups are intense and scented, and contain a high percentage of fruit and little else; the best versions are often Belgian, Swiss, Dutch, French, or German. They come in different flavors, such as peach-passion fruit (pictured), red fruits, or apple and pear, and can be useful in fruit tarts, pies, compotes, fruit salads, and ice cream, matched with similar fruits; drizzle them over cheesecakes or panna cotta.

10 Crème de cassis This intensely sweet but sharp blackcurrant liqueur is totally luscious when folded through thick cream, yogurt, fromage frais, or custard, or drizzled over lemon chocolate or bitter chocolate mousse. In red wine jelly, with berry fruits, it is absolutely glorious.

11 Elderflower cordial The best elderflower cordial, flowery and Muscat-scented, is made by steeping elderflower blossoms in liquid with sugar, lemon juice, and citric acid. It is both sweet and sharp. Use the cordial, diluted, as a drink, or add some to weak black tea instead of lemon. Or try pouring some over fritters or over melon, and use it to dampen cakes in trifle-style desserts, or to sweeten apple puddings.

12 Golden syrup A unique British creation, golden syrup is a more refined product than black treacle. Densely thick, clear, and sweet, it is scrumptious spread on muffins or scones, or poured over suet puddings. It adds an interesting sweetness and moistness to cakes and steamed puddings, and is essential in treacle tart. With butter and cream, it makes fudge sauce. Or mix it with vinegar and spices to brush over meats as a glaze.

13 Caramello liquido This sticky, caramelized sugar syrup gives instant richness, color, and flavor. The best versions are made in Spain or Latin America. Try it trickled into marinades, glazes, and sauces, or whisk it into or drizzle it over yogurt or ricotta for a quick dessert. It suits cinnamon, cloves, dark rum, dried fruits, citrus, and creamy mixtures. Brushed over meat to be roasted, liquid caramel adds curious charm and gloss.

scented stock syrup

Makes 3½ cups

This classic syrup has many uses: as a pastry glaze, to sweeten sour fruit juices, or to pour over sliced fresh fruits. Combine 2 cups superfine or granulated sugar, 2 tablespoons liquid glucose syrup, 2 tablespoons lemon juice, and 2 cups boiling water in a saucepan. Heat, stirring, until it comes to a boil, then simmer for 5 minutes or until clear. Remove from the heat and cool slightly over iced water. While still warm, add a 6-inch strip of lemon zest, and 1 cinnamon stick or vanilla pod, if desired. When quite cold, add 3 tablespoons white rum or schnapps. Pour into a bottle and shake. Kept in a cool, dark place, it lasts for months.

caramelized nuts for praline

Pounded to a powder, or praline, caramelized nuts add great color, taste, and texture to ice cream, yogurt, creamy custards, or plain pastries. Put ½ cup blanched almonds or mixed nuts on to a flexible metal tray. Measure ½ cup granulated sugar into a clean, dry frying pan. Place over high heat and shake the pan horizontally, never stirring (to prevent the formation of crystals), and continue to cook; the base layer will melt first, followed by the upper layer. Turn down the heat to medium-low, and continue to cook, using the same movements, until the caramel turns from pale to medium gold. Carefully pour it over the nuts, and let sit for 3 to 5 minutes to set and cool. Twist the metal tray and splinter off chunks of nut brittle. Pound these to a coarse or fine powder, and store in an airtight container.

steamed ginger puddings

These soft and steamy individual puddings have the unexpected bite of stem ginger in syrup, and golden syrup to sweeten them. Serve with vanilla custard or cream.

Serves 4

Ingredients

9 tablespoons salted butter, softened
½ cup superfine sugar
2 eggs, beaten
1 cup self-rising flour, sifted
1 teaspoon baking powder, sifted
4 tablespoons scented stock syrup (see opposite), or golden syrup (melted)
4 chunks stem ginger, finely sliced
4 teaspoons stem ginger syrup
4 teaspoons golden syrup, maple syrup, or clear honey

Method

1. Have a large steamer ready. Butter four 6-ounce heatproof bowls (non-metal if using a microwave).
2. Cream the butter, sugar, eggs, and 2 tablespoons of the flour together in a medium-sized bowl, using an electric whisk or rotary beater. Add the remaining flour and the baking powder, and gently stir in the scented stock syrup (or golden syrup).
3. Divide the pudding mixture among the prepared bowls. Place the bowls in the steamer and cover all four with one large sheet of oiled aluminum foil. Steam for 25 to 30 minutes, until firm and risen: A metal skewer inserted into one of the puddings should come out clean. (Alternatively, microwave on High for 6 to 8 minutes.)
4. Turn the puddings out onto 4 serving plates. Pile slices of stem ginger on top of each, and drizzle with some of both syrups.

essences and flavored waters

In everyday life, we are often unaware of the significance of aromatics, but a sip of an almond-scented cappuccino or a bite of an orange flower–scented madeleine rarely fails to trigger feelings of comfort and well-being. When using these volatile flavors, however, we must be discreet. Most essences and flavored waters are highly concentrated and should be used in tiny amounts: add them drop by drop, particularly if using strong flavors such as bitter almond. Essences should usually be added late in the cooking process.

1 Bitter almond extract Made from roasted bitter almonds, the essence of which is dissolved out in oil, this concentrated flavoring has a bittersweet and lingering taste. It works well with fruits of the apricot and cherry family, and is the crucial flavor in marzipan, macaroons, and frangipane. Note that plain almond essence is not the same thing.

2 Peppermint oil Clear, intense, and almost medicinal in taste, this flavoring creates a coolness that offsets the sweet, rich taste of chocolate, for example. A few drops can improve fresh fruit salads.

3 Vanilla extract Vanilla pods, macerated in alcohol, create a densely aromatic extract, or essence; beware of those that contain synthetic "vanillin" flavor. Use vanilla extract toward the end of cooking, in ice cream, custards, milky sauces, and puddings.

4 Rose water Steam-distilled from rose petals, rose water is floral and intensely musky. Double- or triple-distilled types are the best buy. Perhaps best known for its use in Turkish delight, rose water also goes well with berries: Try raspberry and rose ice cream, for example.

5 Orange flower water This citrus-sweet liquid, also known as orange blossom water, is distilled from the white blossoms of bitter oranges. Superb in fruit or rice desserts, it also excels in combination with dates, nuts, honey, and yogurt or cream.

6 Tea If using tea as a flavoring, it pays to use a good-quality one. Black and green teas are the most useful. Earl Grey tea (a), a black tea, has an intense, sweet-citrussy appeal and tannic intensity. Brew it in boiling milk as the basis of tea ice cream, or use it in syrups, or to rehydrate dried fruits. Green tea, intensely floral and scented perhaps with passion fruit (b), or hand-rolled and exquisitely delicate (c), can be used as a broth for poaching duck or chicken. Chinese white tea (d) is a fascinating product only recently introduced to Europe, and comes in beautifully hand-twisted shapes. Similar to, but less tannic than, green tea, white tea can be used as a cooking liquid for delicate white meats or fish.

7 Coffee For cooking purposes, coffee is best made from high-quality roasted coffee beans (a), ground at the time of use and brewed using near-boiling water. Select a good blend such as mocha and Java. and use it, fortified, in cakes, creamy mousses, tiramisu-type desserts, or in caramel, butterscotch, and toffee sauces.

Unroasted coffee beans (b) are hard to find, but provide a great flavor when freshly roasted. Put the beans in a heavy-bottom frying pan over medium to high heat, and shake, stir, and turn them regularly; remove when browned and aromatic, and grind them once cooled.

6a

6b

6d

6c

7b

7a

alcohols for sweet flavorings

With relatively little effort, you can use characterful, good-quality alcohols to achieve fascinating complexity and outrageously delicious effects. Use them as you would essences, added little and late for background flavors. Alternatively, you can splash alcohols generously into everything from custards and compotes to jellies, cakes, and preserves. Try to contrast long-aged spirits with the sweet-sharp shock of pineapple, passion fruit, or raspberry. Macerate raisins in rum, make a ginger wine–enriched ganache—the possibilities are endless.

1   2   3   4   5   6   7   8   9

I Bitters These spirit-based tonic mixers, flavored with bitter herbs, roots, and flowers, give a spicy, aromatic bitterness to both sweet and savory dishes: Add a few drops to ice creams, fruit salads, or jellies, or to marinades and stews. Most famous is brick-red Angostura (pictured), traditionally used in pink gin.

2 Gin The herbal intensity of gin goes well with apple and cinnamon dishes, pears in cardamom-scented syrup, black currant desserts, and lemon and orange ices and cheesecakes. Add gin early in cooking, flambé it to evaporate off the alcohol, or add it late to keep its full power.

3 Cognac Brandy is more useful in cooking than any other spirit, and cognac, from France, is as good as brandy gets. It is excellent for flambéed pancakes, it enriches fruit cakes, it helps to preserve jams, and it excels in chocolate, vanilla, coffee, and cream desserts.

4 Ginger wine This spicy wine is made from fortified raisin wine, which is steeped in ground ginger for weeks, and matured for a year. It enriches soups and can be used in glazes for pastries.

5 Cointreau This brandy-based, triple sec spirit is flavored with bitter orange peel and aromatics. Syrupy sweet, citrussy, and herbal, Cointreau is excellent in chocolate-, citrus , and even coffee-flavored desserts. It also works well in cakes, pastries, mousses, and jellies.

6 Dark rum Most commonly distilled from cane-sugar molasses, dark rums are ripe, fruity, and fiery. They can be used in confectionery, syrups, sauces, butters, creams, custards, and ice cream. Drizzled over warm cakes or pastries, or in fruit purees, a combination of rum and citrus zest works wonders. Potent Stroh rum, from Austria, is excellent in plum pastries and sweet sauces.

7 Port The only major fortified wine to be based on red wine, this delicious Portuguese spirit works well in sweet cheese pastries, nut desserts, jellies, and dried fruit dishes, or can be used to fortify jams and compotes.

8 Marsala Available in varying degrees of strength and sweetness, this fortified wine from Sicily is rich, mellow, and sticky, and perfect for many cooking tasks. It is the classic alcohol to use in zabaglione and tiramisu.

9 Sweet sherry Delicious sweet sherry from Spain is essential in English trifle. Amontillado (medium sweet) and oloroso (sweet and intensely rich) can both be drizzled over steam puddings or used in Christmas pudding or fruit cakes. Ladyfingers, soaked in sherry, and layered with hot caramel sauce, nuts, and mascarpone, makes a sensational dessert.

tiramisu

This classic Italian dessert is voluptuously textured, and combines the rich, smoky flavor of fortified wine with the aromas of vanilla and coffee. It is easily achieved using almost all pantry ingredients. Make it quickly just before serving or chill it for up to 8 hours beforehand.

Serves 4

Ingredients

6 tablespoons freshly made hot, strong coffee
8 tablespoons sweet Marsala or Madeira
2 tablespoons dark rum, cognac, or amaretto
1 teaspoon vanilla extract
16 ladyfinger cookies
1¾ pounds mascarpone, beaten until smooth
1 tablespoon cocoa, sifted
1 tablespoon confectioners' sugar, sifted

Method

1. Pour the first four ingredients into a shallow dish, and stir to combine.
2. Quickly dip each ladyfinger into the coffee mixture, and set aside on a piece of aluminum foil.
3. Whisk half of the remaining liquid into half of the mascarpone.
4. Make a crisscross using two dipped ladyfingers in the base of each of 4 serving glasses or dishes. Drizzle with some of the remaining coffee mixture and spoon in some of the flavored mascarpone.
5. Repeat the layering. Spoon the plain mascarpone over the top.
6. Drizzle with any remaining coffee syrup. Combine the cocoa and confectioners' sugar in a small sieve and sift them together over the tiramisu. Serve immediately or chill.

poached fruits in lemon verbena and caramelized seeds

Raymond Blanc, the creative and innovative chef-patron of Le Manoir aux Quat' Saisons, near Oxford, England, devised this refreshing dish, which uses a scented herb tea to infuse delicate flavors and create a light fruit syrup for dried fruits. With some toasted nuts and seeds sprinkled on top, and perhaps a dollop of Greek yogurt, it makes a delicious breakfast or dessert dish.

Serves 4

Ingredients

- 4 tablespoons lemon verbena, chopped, or other herbal tea: jasmine, ginger, or red fruit
- 12 Agen prunes (these have the best flavor and hold their texture when soaked)
- 2 ripe Williams or Comice pears, skin on, core removed, cut lengthwise into 8 pieces
- 1 heaping tablespoon each of sunflower seeds, pine nuts, flax seed, pumpkin seeds, and sliced almonds
- 1 heaping tablespoon maple syrup
- 1 dried fig, flattened with the back of your hand, then finely sliced
- 1 teaspoon finely sliced fresh peppermint or 4 fresh mint sprigs (optional)

Method

1. Bring 1¼ cups of water to a boil and pour it over the lemon verbena or tea and let infuse for 5 minutes. Strain the warm tea over the Agen prunes and let them soak for 8 to 12 hours.

2. Lift the prunes out of the tea using a slotted spoon and set them aside. Pour the soaking liquid into a saucepan, add the pear, cover, bring to a boil and simmer for 30 seconds. If the pears you are using are slightly underripe, cook them for 2 minutes longer. Remove from the heat and let the pears cool in the liquid.

3. To cook the seeds, preheat the oven to 425°F. Combine the seeds with the maple syrup, then spread them on a nonstick baking sheet. Roast in the oven for 8 minutes, or until light golden brown, then set aside. (Toasting the seeds intensifies their flavor; you can also do this under the broiler if necessary.)

4. Divide the caramelized seeds among 4 serving bowls, arrange the poached pears and prunes on top, and scatter the sliced fig over the fruit. Divide the cooking juices among the bowls, and, if you want, scatter the peppermint on top.

spreads, pastes, and conserves

The best types of sweet spreads, pastes, and conserves can widen a cook's repertoire considerably. Because, in most cases water has been evaporated off in the cooking, these foods are usually concentrated and flavorful. The nature of their manufacture also means that they have a long shelf life.

The most desirable spreads and conserves have realistic colors—which may be muted rather than brilliant—and pleasing textures: Nougat, for example, should have a dense, chewy texture rather than a soft and sticky, glucose-boosted consistency; good jams should have an appealing soft consistency, and not be hard and sticky due to the excessive use of setting agents. The best jams are those with refreshingly few ingredients: fruit, sugar, and perhaps citric, tartaric, or ascorbic acid to create a perfect set.

1 Cajeta (dulce de leche) Made by boiling down milk with sugar, this rich caramel is loved in Spain, Portugal, and Latin America; you may also find it labeled "manjar blanco." Scandinavians and the French produce a similar product, known as "milk jam." It is superb spread on sweet pancakes or toasted brioches, or folded into yogurt or cream cheese. Whisked with milk, it makes an instant caramel shake.

2 Povidl plum paste This concentrated plum jam paste, flavored with dark rum, is a favorite in Viennese dishes and is well worth seeking out. It can be used as a topping or heated with juice as an intensely flavored sauce, which is excellent with cakes, pancakes, and ice creams. Use it with ground poppy seeds or apple to fill pastry tartlets.

3 Membrillo (quince paste) This sticky, intensely sweet-sharp fruit "cheese" results from the long-cooking of quince with sugar. Superb served with blue cheeses, it can also be dissolved in sweet wine and folded through soft cheese with saffron and honey as a dessert. Dice it up and bake in pastry shells for instant fruit pies, or add it to citrus fruit salads. Guava paste is a Central American equivalent.

4 Halva This name covers a wide range of Middle Eastern, Central Asian, Turkish, and Greek sweetmeats. The most common type of halva found in Europe is made of ground sesame seeds and sugar syrup or honey, flavored with nuts, candied fruits, and spices. It is delicious crushed into ice cream or used to fill dried figs, dates, and peaches.

5 Pavé de fruits These concentrated, sugar-coated pastes are made by boiling down the juice of naturally sharp fruits, such as black currants, with sugar. These are excellent as petit fours with slivers of Parmesan pressed on top. Finely chopped, stirred into mascarpone, and drizzled with Marsala, they make a quick and elegant dessert.

6 Nougat Known as nougat in English and French, *turrón* in Spanish, and *torrone* in Italian, this intensely sweet paste is made of boiled honey and/or sugar syrup mixed with egg whites, nuts, vanilla, and candied fruits. Use it crumbled into ice cream or crushed on scented fresh figs or ripe peaches, or layer it into a dense cake with membrillo.

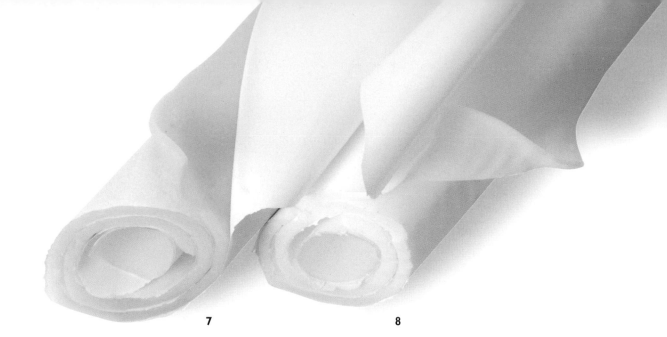

7   **8**

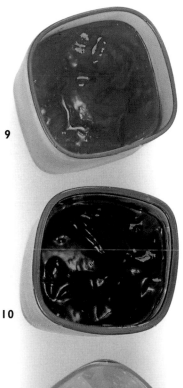

9

10

11

12

7 Marzipan This beautifully textured almond and sugar paste can be bought in convenient blocks or rolls. Startlingly yellow marzipan used to be the norm, but now more natural shades are also available. Integral to certain traditional recipes, such as stollen and simnel cake, marzipan is also used to separate a fruit cake from its royal icing (see below). It makes a good filling for pastries and chocolates, and can be colored and layered for sweetmeats.

8 Royal icing Blocks and rolls of icing are good for speed and easy application—particularly when covering Christmas or wedding cakes. Try making it more interesting by brushing on flavorings (such as rose water or orange flower water), or by adding color, or even gold or silver leaf.

9 Apricot jam Sharp, sweet-scented, and almondy, apricot jam is an indispensable pantry ingredient. Melted with lemon juice and strained, it makes a superb golden glaze for use on apple and pear tarts. Spoon it over cream cheese and serve with langues-de-chat biscuits, or fold it into whipped cream for an apricot fool.

10 Red currant jelly This strained fruit jelly preserve is soft but firm, sharp but fruity sweet. It melts easily with lemon juice to form a glaze that sets on cooling: It is excellent for berry and currant

pastries, and plum or peach tarts. Serve it melted over fresh red currants, with fromage frais or cream cheese, as a dessert.

11 Lemon curd This custardy, intensely lemony preserve, sometimes known as lemon cheese or lemon butter, is perfect spread on hot toast, scones, or toasted muffins, but is surprisingly useful to cook with, too. It is delicious in a pavlova, covered in whipped cream or with passion fruit pulp and orange flower water folded in. Mixed with mashed bananas and yogurt it makes a quick fruit fool. Diluted with lemon juice or white wine, it can be used as a sauce for ice cream.

12 Fruit compote Made of fruit stewed with sugar and water, compotes often go to a mush—particularly if fruits such as greengage plums, rhubarb, or apricots are used. Other fruits, such as forest fruits or red fruits (pictured), tend to hold their shape better. When buying compotes, look for a natural color: The fruits should retain their subtle, natural tones.

Compotes are very useful for making quick desserts. Use them in fruit pies, or fools, or pureed in yogurt drinks, or eat them straight with cream and fine crisp wafers. Or try layering the fruit with yogurt, or setting it, using gelatin, to a jelly. Vanilla, cinnamon, or citrus zest can be added to forest fruit compotes for extra flavor.

white chocolate sauce with mint

"The mint adds freshness to this sauce, which is ideal for making a marriage of two chocolate sauces with a selection of all-chocolate desserts. It is also delicious served over dark chocolate ice cream with a few pistachios scattered on top," says Michel Roux, chef-patron of the famous Waterside Inn, at Bray-on-Thames, England. His superb intense sauce maximizes the flavors in a very effective way.

Serves 6

Ingredients
9 ounces white couverture or
    best-quality white chocolate,
    chopped
¾ cup milk
6 tablespoons plus 2 teaspoons
    heavy cream
¼ cup fresh mint leaves
¾ teaspoon caraway seeds

Method
1. Put the white chocolate in a bowl set over a saucepan of gently simmering water over low heat; stir with a wooden spoon until smooth and melted.
2. In a separate saucepan, bring the milk and cream to a boil. As soon as it begins to bubble, toss in the mint leaves and caraway, turn off the heat, and cover the pan.
3. Let infuse for 10 minutes, then pour the milk through a conical sieve onto the melted chocolate. Mix with a whisk until thoroughly combined.
4. Transfer the chocolate sauce to a clean saucepan, set over medium heat, and let simmer for a few seconds, whisking continuously.
5. Serve the sauce hot. If you are not serving it immediately, you can keep it warm in a bain-marie for a few minutes.

chocolate brownie cakes

These superb little soufflélike cakes contain bitter chocolate, which trickles forth temptingly when they are cut. Serve either plain or with ice-cold crème fraîche.

Serves 4

Ingredients

4 tablespoons plus 1 teaspoon salted butter, cut into pieces

4½ ounces bittersweet chocolate, preferably at least 60% cocoa solids, chopped

2 medium eggs, at room temperature

2 medium egg yolks, at room temperature

3 tablespoons vanilla sugar

4 teaspoons flour

½ teaspoon ground cinnamon

confectioners' sugar, for dusting (optional)

Method

1. Put ¼ cup of the butter and all the chocolate in the top half of and melt completely over low heat. (Alternatively, microwave on High for intervals of 30 seconds, no longer, until melted.) Beat to mix.

2. In a separate bowl, whisk together the eggs, egg yolks, and vanilla sugar, using an electric beater, until light, pale, and thick.

3. Pour the egg mixture, 2 teaspoons of the flour, and the cinnamon into the chocolate-butter mixture.

4. Using the remaining butter, coat four 6-ounce metal molds, heatproof ramekins, or heatproof glass dishes. Dust in the reserved flour. Repeat this process. Spoon the chocolate brownie mix equally into the dishes.

5. Bake in an oven preheated to 450°F, for 6 to 7 minutes, or until the top and sides look and feel set.

6. Let the cakes sit for 1 minute. Tip each one gently on its side, and with your fingers ease each cake out onto a plate: It should be complete. Dust with confectioners' sugar, if desired, and serve hot.

4 Chocolate chips You should always look for good-quality chocolate, even when buying chips. Fast to melt and superbly convenient, chips can be coarsely chopped and dropped, at the last minute, into muffin batters and doughs. Or use them whole, melted into sauces.

5 Chocolate rounds Though much harder to find than chocolate chips (but of reliably better quality), cup-shaped chocolate rounds can be used in similar ways. Try crushing them into pleasingly chunky or jagged pieces. They are a great addition to ice creams.

6 Chocolate paste A world away from the ultrasweet chocolate spreads aimed at children, this intense, dense, and creamy paste is made by melting bitter chocolate in cream. You may find it sold as "ganache" or even "truffle paste."

The paste is normally liquid at room temperature and solidifies if refrigerated. You can use it as a spread for cakes, or, gently heated, as a sauce. Rolled into balls and coated with cocoa, it is transformed into truffles.

7 Cocoa During processing, once all of the cocoa butter has been removed, the pure cocoa mass, further roasted and ground, becomes cocoa. The best cocoa should be unsweetened and have a high (100 percent) cocoa solids content. Gastronomic cocoa (a) is superbly dark, intense, aromatic, and bitter—as well as expensive. It can be used as you would use either chocolate or cocoa. Melt it in cream, butter, or alcohol for intense sauces, desserts, ganache, truffles. or chocolate fillings.

The most flavorful cocoas are usually those produced in France or Holland. It was a Dutchman who, in the nineteenth century, pioneered the process for alkali-treating cocoa in order to modify its excessive natural acidity. This resulted in a darker-colored but milder cocoa, which also dissolved more easily in water. To this day, Dutch-process cocoa (b) is an alkali-treated, often deep mauve-brown cocoa with a sweet aroma and mellow taste. It dissolves easily and usually clumps little.

British cocoa (c), also alkali-treated, tends to be lighter colored but is full of flavor and good for everyday use.

Use cocoa as a flavoring for cakes, cookies, brownies, and butter icings, for dusting creamy desserts, or coating sweetmeats. Cooked with honey, cream, and brandy, or simply with sugar in water or cream, it can produce an intense and shiny sauce.

8 Pressed cocoa cakes These curious cakes are made from fermented cocoa, and are minimally processed. They give an intense chocolate flavor. Grate them for cocoa, or melt them in cream for cooked dishes. You are most likely to find them in spice shops or ethnic grocers.

melting chocolate

To melt chocolate, break it up into a bowl and place it over a saucepan of boiling water. Or, use the microwave and heat the chocolate in fifteen-second bursts. If the chocolate gets too hot, it spoils. White chocolate, in particular, needs slow and careful melting. Whichever chocolate you use, add any other liquids (such as cream or alcohol) at the start. While butter or cream make chocolate more silky and manageable, watery liquids or alcohol, added once it has melted, may cause it to "seize" (become hard and grainy).

chocolate

The raw material from which chocolate is made, the cocoa bean, comes in several varieties. Each has its own distinct aroma and flavor, which develops when the bean is fermented and roasted. Heat generated during the subsequent grinding melts the bean's natural cocoa butter, which is released in a liquid known as the cocoa mass or chocolate liquor. This cocoa mass, consisting of cocoa butter and cocoa solids, is the essential ingredient in the manufacture of chocolate. The amount of sugar added (and whether milk is also added) before further refining determines what type of chocolate it is to become.

I Dark chocolate Dark, or plain, chocolate comes in many different grades: In continental Europe and North America, it is subdivided into "sweet," "semisweet," "bitter-sweet," and "unsweetened" types. Bittersweet chocolate has very little sugar added and is the perfect cooking chocolate. Always look for a high cocoa solids content, at least 60 to 70 percent. Chefs use French couverture chocolate, which is designed for coating and icing; it has high levels of cocoa butter and is specially treated in order to create plasticity and a high gloss. At home, you can add cream or butter to high–cocoa solids chocolate to make it more pliable.

Dark chocolate makes superb ganache (half chocolate and half cream, melted together), which sets semihard and is excellent for coating nuts, cookies, or cakes, or for molding into chocolates. Or cook it with light cream, dark rum, and cinnamon as a sauce for ice cream, cakes. and pears. Good-quality unsweetened chocolate, melted into mole or turkey gravy, adds class, richness, and color.

2 White chocolate Most chocolate aficionados rate this as an inferior product. It is hardly chocolate at all, since it contains no cocoa mass, just cocoa butter, sugar, and condensed milk. Mainly used for color contrast and texture, white chocolate can be cloying if it is not tempered by other ingredients such as orange or lemon. Swirl it into melted milk or dark chocolate for marbled chocolate coatings or to add interest to brownies. Make ganache, and roll it into balls, to be coated in cocoa for truffles. Or use it for vanilla and white chocolate ice cream.

3 Milk chocolate With added condensed milk and lots of extra sugar, milk chocolate's cocoa solids content drops to 20 to 30 percent. Crucially, the taste and texture of the chocolate is determined by the additions: Look for a chocolate that contains real cocoa butter or good CBEs—cocoa butter equivalents, common in mass-produced milk chocolate—such as lecithin, and not vegetable fat. Milder than dark chocolate but still, ideally, distinctively chocolatey, milk chocolate can be pleasant to use in cooking, depending on your tastes. Use it as for dark chocolate, but expect a rather more subtle cocoa "hit." Try melting it, straight, to coat marshmallows, cookies, or nuts such as Brazil nuts or almonds.

choosing good chocolate

The higher the percentage of cocoa solids, the stronger the chocolate flavor will be. However, a high cocoa solids content is just one element of a good chocolate; the way in which the beans are processed is also vitally important. Most chocolate is sweetened to some extent, but the lower the sugar content, the better it will be to cook with.

sweet cookies

Home-baked cookies are, of course, delicious, but some cookies are difficult to reproduce at home, especially those with lacy, brittle, or chewy textures. The classic cookies and confections described here are made using good ingredients and can be used to create desserts in minutes.

1 Langues-de-chat These wafer-thin French cookies line molded fruit charlottes beautifully, and can be used to line ice cream molds, or to sandwich tiny slices of ice cream. Layered with crème chantilly and pureed apricot, they make superb desserts.

2 Speculaas These crunchy Dutch cookies are flavored with ginger and cardamom. (Similar spicy cookies exist all over Europe.) They can be used in trifles, crumbled between apples and yogurt, or finely crushed and folded into crème fraîche.

3 Gingersnaps Delicately thin and spicy, these cookies can be crushed over baked fruits, crumbled for use in cheesecakes, or mixed with yogurt and preserved ginger.

4 Amaretti These famous cookies, wrapped in pairs, have a distinctive bitter almond taste and are superb in cooking. Soaked in Marsala and layered with ricotta, they make an instant pudding. Crumble them to top baked or fresh peaches, or add them as a crunchy topping to pureed apricots with mascarpone.

5 Ladyfingers Also known as boudoir or savoiardi cookies, these puffy but crisp sponge cookies are perfect for soaking up alcohol: in trifles (dipped first into port or sherry) and tiramisu (dipped into coffee liqueur), for example.

6 Brandysnap baskets These lacy, toffeelike wafers, which can be rolled (brandysnaps) or shaped into baskets, can be filled with all sorts of delicious things, from simple whipped cream to diced pears or rum-soaked soft berries. Brushed with melted chocolate, they'll hold chocolate mousse or ice cream.

7 Marshmallows Fluffy, soft, and bland, these sweet confections are a common cooking ingredient in the United States, for cakes and sweet sauces. Try folding them into melted chocolate and mixing with nuts for a rich dessert.

8 Digestive biscuits Made with whole meal flour, these high-fiber cookies have a "short," crumbly texture that is perfect for crushing for cheesecake and Banoffee pie bases. Also try them crumbled with nuts, rolled oats, and butter as a baked fruit topping.

9 Biscotti Literally "twice cooked," these Italian cookies usually contain nuts, dried fruit, or chocolate, and work beautifully in frothy egg or cream desserts. Use them, alcohol-dipped, as a basis for trifles. Crushed and softened in vin santo and mixed with ricotta and ground coffee beans, they make a scrumptious pudding.

10 Meringues These confections of egg white and sugar, though easily made, take hours to cook. Ready-made meringues are perfectly good for making ice cream sundaes or Eton Mess (crushed meringue and raspberries folded into heavy cream).

preserved
fruit &
vegetables

dried fruit

Sweet, energy-packed, and long-lasting, dried fruit are one of nature's most dazzling convenience foods. Totally versatile, they are useful in innumerable dishes, from puddings—soaked in fruit juice or alcohol, dried fruit make elegant desserts—to salads and rice dishes. Once upon a time, all we could buy were raisins, prunes, and apricots, but now the choice is huge and infinitely colorful.

Avoid overdried fruits, which can't be improved by hours of soaking, though now the fashion is more for dried fruits that are soft and "ready to eat." Most fruits, when dried, don't retain their color and moisture naturally, so are coated or soaked in substances that may or may not be acceptable: always check the label. (Sulfur dioxide, used on a lot of ready-to-eat products, helps retain the fruit's color and natural acidity but it may cause allergic reactions in asthmatics.)

1 Raisins Juicy dried grapes, raisins vary in shape, size, flavor, and seed content, depending on the grape type used. Many come from California and are seedless, dark, small, and glossy (a). Use these in dried fruit salads, muffins, stuffed apples, and chutneys. Muscat raisins (b), made from the supersweet Muscat grape, keep some of the original bloom and are sharp-tasting. These can be plumped up in cinnamon-tea syrup, mixed with cream cheese, and drizzled with muscatel wine, or used in rum and raisin ice cream. Jumbo or golden raisins are superb in rice puddings, cheesecakes, and other dishes where their pale color counts.

2 Sultanas Made from dried seedless green grapes, sultanas are paler and sweeter than raisins. Their color and flavor changes according to their provenance. Some suit certain uses better than others, but Californian (a), Australian (b), and South African (c) sultanas, for example, are all good in sponge puddings, sweet pastries, fruit cakes, spice breads, cookies, curries and chutneys.

3 Currants Originally from Corinth in Greece, currants are one of the most ancient of dried vine fruits. They are tiny black grapes that, when dried, are intensely sweet but very tart. They are much used in baking, including in dried fruit mixtures for mincemeat pastries.

4 Prunes Dark, glossy, and chewy, prunes are simply dried plums. Californian prunes (a) dominate the market. While the ready-to-eat versions are perfect for stuffing with blanched almonds or cream cheese, the drier versions usually need simmering in water, wine, or port, for use in meat stews, mousses and compotes. The sexiest prunes around are the plump Agen prunes (b), from France, best eaten on their own or wrapped in bacon and grilled.

5 Dates The dried fruits of a type of palm tree, and a staple food in North Africa and the Middle East, are either "soft" (eaten fresh), "semi-dry" (the most common), or "hard" (rare in the West). Use semi-dry dates (a) in loaves, cookies, and steamed puddings, or cook them with orange juice to a puree for filling cakes. Fleshy Medjool dates (b), also semi-dry, are delicious eaten uncooked and filled with cheese, nuts, or marzipan. Or mix them with orange flower water and sliced orange, as a salad.

6 Sour cherries These are deliciously scented, sweet, and sharp, and grow fat, soft, and juicy when soaked. Use them in sauces, steamed puddings, and pie fillings, or soak them in kirsch for cheesecakes.

7 Cranberries Sweet but sharp, dried cranberries add pleasing tartness and color to all kinds of sweet and savory foods, especially rice and yogurt dishes, spiced pastries, and fruit compotes. Try them in rich apple tart for contrast, or cook and then puree them with spiced syrup for sweet pastries.

8 Barberries These gloriously red, jewel-like fruit have a clean, sharp flavor and are a favorite Middle Eastern food. Add them to sweet rice dishes and yogurt or cream cheese desserts, or scatter them over stewed fruits for texture, color, and acidity.

9 Apricots Dried apricots have glorious sharp-scented sweetness, color, and chewiness. Cooked, in pies or as a puree with orange flower water, or to stir into creamy desserts, they excel. For many cooks, the bright orange, sweet-

sharp apricots (a) are the ideal. The more healthful unsulfured versions are a dark brown and have a toffeelike flavor. Dried apricots are also available in pieces (b).

10 Amardine (apricot paste sheet) Of Middle Eastern and eastern Mediterranean origin, amardine can be cut into shapes, or rolled up with marzipan as sweet sushi. Or boil it with orange juice, add sugar and orange flower water, and blend to make a drink.

11 Coconut The white meat of the coconut is available dried in various forms. Coconut flakes (a), thin slivers of coconut, are excellent mixed with brown sugar, butter, and nuts as a topping for baked fruit puddings. Use them in muffins and banana loaves, or toast and crumble them over raw seafood or ceviche.

More common desiccated coconut (b), a powdery product, is useful for coconut cakes and ice cream, and to thicken curries (it is very absorbent); buy the plain rather than the sweetened version.

12 Figs Many types of dried and semi-dried figs are produced all over the Mediterranean. They are usually sold either whole (a) or

pressed into cakes, which are easily broken up into individual figs (b). Because of the high sugar content, figs dry superbly well. They are wonderful in chutneys, sauces, and pickles, and add lemony sweetness to stews, cakes, and puddings. Miniature, white figs (c) are good added whole to meat and poultry marinades, or rehydrated in hot liquids to add to salads.

13 Fruit leathers Antipodean fruit leathers, made from dried red berry or stone fruit puree, are strong, sharp, and sweet. They can be cut up with scissors and heated in water or wine to make a sauce, or used to add brilliant fruit flavor and color to cakes and puddings.

fruited turkey and chestnut meat loaf

This meat loaf uses minced turkey and pork in place of the usual minced beef, and has dried fruits and chestnuts to add a boost to the flavor and texture. The result is an intriguing mosaic of lean meat and fruit. Served hot, the loaf is a wonderful, celebratory autumn or winter dish, but it is also delicious served cold.

Serves 4–6

Ingredients

Olive oil, for brushing
1 pound minced lean turkey dark meat
¼ pound minced lean pork or minced bacon
2 tablespoons concentrated chicken bouillon
1 handful parsley and/or mixed fresh herbs, chopped, or 2 teaspoons dried herbs
2 tablespoons Worcestershire sauce
1 teaspoon anchovy paste
5 ounces dried apricots or peaches
5 ounces Agen prunes
3 ounces dried cranberries, cherries, or blueberries
1 slice whole wheat or granary bread, pulled into crumbs
1 egg, beaten
7 ounces canned or vac-packed chestnuts
½ pound turkey strips
Salt and freshly ground black pepper

Method

1. Fold a large piece of aluminum foil in half and use it to line the base and two long sides of a 9-by-5-by-3-inch metal loaf pan. Leave extra foil at the sides to wrap over the top as the loaf cooks. Brush or rub the whole surface (including the short ends of the pan) with the oil.
2. Mix the turkey, pork, and bouillon in a bowl. Add the herbs, Worcestershire sauce, and anchovy paste.
3. Pour ½ cup boiling water over the dried fruits. Let soak for 10 minutes, then drain, reserving 4 tablespoons of the soaking liquid. Mix the liquid with the bread crumbs and beat with a fork. Stir the beaten egg and then the soaked bread into the meat mixture.
4. Using scissors, cut 4 each of the apricots, prunes, and chestnuts, and add them along with several of the smaller fruits to the meat mixture.
5. Use some of the remaining fruits and chestnuts to line the bottom of the loaf pan. Press in one-third of the meat mixture, then some turkey strips, and more dried fruit and chestnuts. Repeat the process until all the ingredients are used up. Press the mixture down firmly with wetted hands, and fold the oiled foil flaps over the top, loosely.
6. Bake in an oven, preheated to 350°F, for 50 to 60 minutes, opening the foil after 40 minutes. Test the interior temperature, using a meat thermometer: it should be 160°F or so. Remove from the oven and let the loaf stand for 10 minutes.
7. Drain off any liquid that has accumulated. (This will turn into jelly by the next day, and can be served cold with the loaf, or used in soup.) Serve the loaf in thick slices, hot (or chilled, the next day).

abricotines

The elegantly minimalist recipe for these sweets features in Claudia Roden's wonderful work *The Book of Jewish Food*. To get the best results, follow her advice about choosing the fruit: "Make these with a natural—tart—variety of dried apricots, not the sweetened or honeyed ones. They must also be soft."

Makes 56

Ingredients
1 pound dried apricots
½ cup pistachios, coarsely chopped
Confectioners' sugar, for coating
A few whole pistachios, for garnish

Method
1. Do not soak or wash the apricots. Put them as they are in a food processor and blend them to a smooth paste, adding a very little water, by the teaspoon, if necessary.
2. Work the chopped pistachios into the paste with your hands.
3. Wash your hands and, wetting them or greasing them with a little oil so that the paste does not stick, take little lumps of paste and roll it into marble-sized balls.
4. Roll them in confectioners' sugar and press half a pistachio on top of each.

foods preserved in sugar or alcohol

Preservation in syrup or alcohol is usually an excellent way to conserve the plumpness and flavor of fruit, vegetables, and other foods. Depending on the sweetness, flavor, and shape of the original foods, they can be either eaten as they are (with yogurt, ice cream, or rice pudding, for example), or used as part of a dessert, whether in a soufflé or tart, or as a filling for pancakes or sweet omelets. Furthermore, the surrounding aromatic liquid is itself useful, in both sweet and savory cooking: Try using it to deglaze the pan after roasting meat, or to add to casseroles or soups.

1 Preserved ginger in syrup These fleshy, sweet-but-hot chunks of fresh ginger in syrup are great for both savory and sweet dishes. You can pour the syrup over ice cream, or use it to flavor custards and yogurts, and ginger can be added to cakes, cookies, or to citrus fruit salads. If you use up the syrup before the ginger, top up the jar with honey or rum.

2 Pears in wine Rosy from being soaked in Ruby Port, pears make excellent festive preserves to serve with game, goose, or ham, or they can be stuffed with cheese or nuts as an easy dessert. Boiled down until it is sticky, the preserving liquid becomes intensely flavorful.

3 Glyka A product of Greece and Turkey, *glyka* consists of a sweet, heavy syrup in which tiny immature fruits, such as cherries and figs (pictured), are preserved whole. Beautiful, chewy, and very sweet, these are an acquired taste; you may prefer to add extra acidity. Try them with yogurt or cream cheese.

4 Clementines in alcohol Tiny oranges, such as clementines, flavor any syrup deliciously, particularly if cognac, curaçao, or whiskey is added. Use the fruit and syrup in trifles or rice puddings, or stir them into thick cream.

5 Cherries in alcohol Dark cherries preserve wonderfully in a syrup containing kirsch or white rum. Use the cherries in ice cream sundaes, in cakes, pavlova, or cheesecakes, or top the cherries and syrup with cream or yogurt as a simple dessert. The syrup flavors smoothies superbly too.

6 Aduki beans These tiny reddish beans, very popular in Thailand, come in a sticky-sweet and nutty syrup. The beans, mashed, can be used to fill dumplings, for steaming, which can then be served with the bean syrup. Or try whizzing the syrup up with lychee juice and rose water, add the lychees and aduki beans, and serve as a drink-cum-dessert on ice.

7 Candied orange slices These colorful slices of orange, pretty as stained-glass windows, can be used to top cheesecakes, orange cakes, or lemon tarts, or to line steamed pudding bowls. Poached in wine, and then reduced, they make an ambrosial pour-over sauce.

8 Marrons glacés Sweet chestnuts, infused with a syrup and usually French, taste superb eaten with Camembert or Roquefort cheese. Or try crumbling them on top of cream, custard, yogurt, or rose-scented rice pudding.

9 Candied citron These colorful pieces of zest, from a large, lemonlike citrus fruit called citron, are infused in syrup until they become dense, leathery, and amazingly sweet. Use slivers to top fruit cakes or milky puddings, or in cream cheese desserts and cheesecakes. Or offer with goat's cheese and walnuts as a salad or dessert in itself. Look for whole pieces rather than the more common fragments.

chutneys, relishes, and sweet pickles

Although precise definitions vary greatly from one food culture to another, salt, vinegar, sugar, and spices underpin most of the products in this category. Hot oils may also feature. These condiments add flavor, texture, crunch, and pungency to rich or plain foods, and make everyday meals more interesting. Mango chutney with a curry, sweet corn relish with a burger, or ploughman's pickle in a cheese sandwich: these pairings typify a lively culinary tradition.

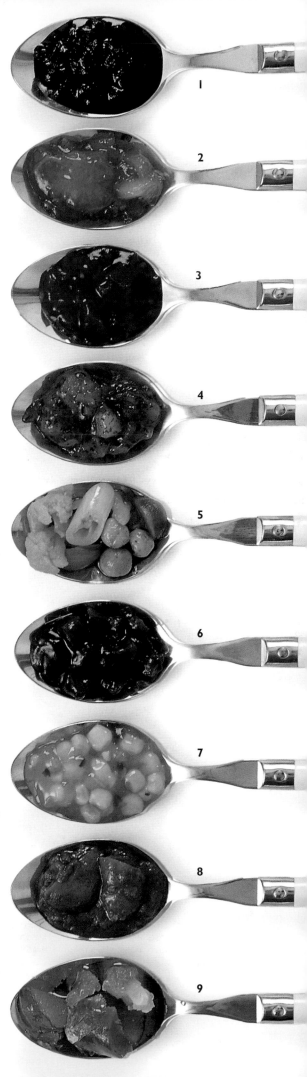

1 Cranberry relish This jamlike relish is a traditional accompaniment for turkey, chicken, or venison. Blend it with equal quantities of orange juice to make an appealing coulis. It also goes extremely well with salty white cheeses, such as feta.

2 Mango chutney The mango chutney so beloved in Britain is not an authentic Indian preserve, despite being a traditional accompaniment to curries. It is sweet and sour rather than hot, turmeric, ginger, and garlic being the usual flavorings. Mango chutney goes well in Cheddar cheese sandwiches and in cold chicken salads. It also adds "bite" to mango ice cream.

3 Tomato and onion chutney Often served with hamburgers or with cold meats or sausages, this sweet relish has only mild spiciness. Whisk it into two parts of softened butter as a barbecue baste for chops and steaks, or stir it into whipped cream as a dressing.

4 Mint and coriander relish This green, herb-rich preserve is a useful accompaniment for many Asian foods, particularly Thai and Vietnamese dishes. Stir it into thick yogurt as a dressing, mix it into fish salads, or serve it with noodle or rice dishes, and coconutty curries.

5 Achards These curious pickles, found in various forms in Africa, India, and Southeast Asia, are made of crunchy, chunky bits of vegetable preserved in a turmeric-flavored pickle liquid. Use them with sliced cold meats, poultry, or fish, or to add interest to noodles and rice. The pickle liquid is also good in Asian vinaigrettes.

6 Ploughman's pickle Apple, onion, and raisins usually feature in this sweet and spicy pickle. Far from subtle, it is an excellent condiment for hard British cheeses, such as Cheddar, and sausages. Mixed into sour cream with paprika, it makes a dip for chicory or apple segments.

7 Sweet corn relish Sweet and mild, this fine-cut, syrupy relish makes a good spread for hot or cold meat sandwiches. It also goes well with cheese, poultry, salami, and smoked fish, such as mackerel. Folded into cottage cheese, it makes a tangy toast-topping or filling for celery sticks.

8 Lime pickle This sharp and spicy Indian pickle is usually fairly dry, with large chunks of lime and other vegetables in a turmeric, chile, and ginger paste. It is superb served as a side dish, with dhal, rice, curries, and pappadoms, or as a refreshing, chewy foil for mild meats, poultry, and fish. Stir it into a mayonnaise-based chicken salad, or add it to ham, tongue, or egg sandwiches.

9 Mostarda di frutta di Cremona This Italian preserve of whole candied fruits in syrup flavored with spicy mustard oil is delicious spooned over slices of rare beef, smoked duck breast, or smoked venison. Mixed with hot roast chicken pan drippings, it creates a delicious and unusual gravy.

pickles

The use of cornichons in sauce tartare, of umeboshi plums in Japanese sushi, and of salt-pickled lemons in Tunisian tagines has been famous for centuries. Dependent on salt, vinegar, and aromatics, pickles pep up our meals, whether they are used alone as condiments or in recipes. They encourage good digestion, stimulate the palate, and keep our interest aroused.

1 Dill pickles and gherkins Small varieties of cucumber, as well as gherkins, are used for pickling. Dill pickles (a) consist of small cucumbers pickled with dill heads or seeds, peppercorns, and other aromatics. Soft, mild, and faintly crunchy, these go well with hard cheese and cured meats, such as pastrami and salami. The pickle liquid is also excellent added to vinaigrettes, or to sour cream to accompany smoked salmon.

Pickled gherkins or, in French, cornichons (b), are smaller, darker and chewier. Eat them with rich pâté and cold meats, or slice them finely as a garnish or to scatter over creamy fish or poultry dishes, to add color and sharpness.

2 Capers The pickled buds of the Mediterranean shrub *Capparis spinosa* come in different sizes. Tiny nonpareils (a) are the most prized, and most enjoyable for their prettiness and sweet, sharp, but mellow flavor. Use them in velouté or béchamel sauces for delicate white fish or poached chicken, or scatter them over mayonnaise-dressed foods. Capucines (b), with a loose, hoodlike outer covering, are medium-sized and good for more general use: on pizzas and in sauces such as salsa verde, tartare sauce, and tapenade. Salted capers (c) can

boost pasta or meat sauces, and are good with skate and black butter sauce, or pounded into herb or French dressings.

Caperberries (d), the fruits of the same plant, are fleshier, milder, and sturdier than the buds. They look and taste good with hard cheeses, ham, salami, and chicken. Remove the stem before chopping or blending them into mayonnaise, hollandaise sauce (for fish), or cream (for poached chicken).

3 Sauerkraut This famous German condiment is essentially dry-salted white cabbage that is preserved by its own fermentation and flavored with spices. Use it straight, hot or cold, as a side dish, or try cooking it with apples and white wine to accompany boiled pork.

4 Baby beets Young beets, preserved in a vinegary brine, are deliciously sweet-sharp and

colorful. Use them to accompany cured herring or, along with onion rings and dill, to embellish open sandwiches. They go well with Dutch cheeses, cold ham, and smoked sausage. Blended to a puree with buttermilk, some pickling liquid, sliced onion, and radishes, they make an instant borscht. Beet salsa with tomato and dill takes just seconds to make.

5 Umeboshi plums The *ume* in *umeboshi* is, in fact, a type of apricot, but because it reddens and grows sourer when pickled, the name "plum" has stuck. Umeboshi are eaten daily in Japan, usually with breakfast rice porridge. Use them, chopped or mashed, in sushi or pureed as a dipping sauce.

6 Preserved lemons Pickled in coarse salt, brine, and aromatics, decorative North African preserved lemons gain an intense, sharp, spicy taste as they mature. (Beware any preserved lemons containing sodium benzoate, which creates off flavors.) Scrape out and discard the pith and the flesh: Only the yellow zest is eaten. Use with couscous, in tagines, or as a stuffing for chicken.

7 Pickled ginger This Japanese condiment consists of paper-thin slices of ginger preserved in a sweet and sour pickle that contains shiso leaf (pink) coloring or beet liquid. It is the traditional

accompaniment for sushi and sashimi, along with wasabi paste and tamari. Pickled ginger can also be used in stir-fries and fish dishes.

8 Pickled samphire Found around Europe, in salt marshes and estuaries near the sea, this slender plant is delicious fresh, but is more often sold pickled, as marsh samphire (or *salicornia*). Pickled samphire makes an unusual condiment, salad, or side dish for salted or smoked seafood. Or use it as a stuffing or sandwich filling for ham or bacon.

9 Mustard greens Pickled mustard greens, of which there are many different variations all over China, have an evil aroma but taste delicious as a condiment. Many are made from

brassicas, such as bok choy or choy sum, and sometimes radish is included. Use them with rice or noodle dishes, or in stuffings for spring rolls, rice paper wraps, or steamed buns.

10 Pickled walnuts These black, sharp-tasting orbs are immature walnuts that have been pickled in a seasoned vinegar. Chewy and astringent, they make a good foil for rich meats, such as roast goose or duck, or strong cheeses. Chop them into pale chicken, rice, or pasta salads for contrast, or wrap them in cured ham and puff pastry, and then bake: superb.

11 Torshi left These luminous pink turnip pieces, in a sharp, sweet beet pickling liquid, are famous in Egypt, Syria, and Lebanon. They have a superb spiciness and applelike crunch. Try them in flatbread wraps, with white cheese, chiles, and lettuce; in a chickpea or lentil salad with rice, cilantro, and olive oil; or in an onion and beet salad with toasted cumin seeds.

12 Kimchi To Koreans, this spicy, sour-tasting pickled cabbage is an essential condiment. There are numerous variations using vegetables such as radish or cucumber, but true kimchi contains only napa cabbage. Kimchi is delicious served with beef and veal dishes, tofu stir-fries, squid, and noodles. The pickle ingredients themselves—including ginger, red chiles, and preserved oysters and/or shrimp—lend particular pungency.

chicken tagine with preserved lemons

This somewhat Westernized North African stew is beautifully fragrant with fruits, spices, and exotic flavorings, shot through with the sharp and spicy intensity of the preserved lemons.

Serves 4–6

Ingredients

14 ounces boneless, skinless chicken thigh fillets, halved

1 onion, cut into eighths, root ends intact

4 tablespoons chermoula spice paste (see page 14)

2 teaspoons turmeric powder

2 tablespoons extra-virgin olive oil or argan oil

8 each of dried figs, apricots, and mango slices

1 apple or pear, cut into segments and cored

2 cups boiling chicken stock or water

2 tablespoons dried rose petals (optional)

1 preserved lemon, in quarters

½ teaspoon rose water or orange flower water

Salt

Method

1. Rub the chicken and onion segments all over with the chermoula and turmeric.

2. Heat the oil in a large heatproof nonreactive pan, add the chicken and onion and cook over medium-high heat until well browned on all sides. Add the dried fruits, apple, stock, and rose petals, if using.

3. Scrape away and discard the flesh and pith from the preserved lemon. Add the rinds to the pan and bring the contents to near boiling, then lower the heat and simmer for 25 to 35 minutes, until the juices are syrupy, the chicken tender, the fruit soft, and the flavors well integrated.

4. Season well with salt: The sweetness needs balancing. Serve hot, with couscous tossed with a little argan oil, salt, and black pepper.

fruit fool in filo pastry cups

The appeal of these delicate desserts depends on the crispness of the filo pastry and the lightness of the creamy filling, which is enlivened by the intense fruit flavors of the vodka-infused black currants.

Serves 4

Ingredients

1 large sheet filo pastry
2 tablespoons salted butter, melted
1 teaspoon scented clear honey
1 (100-gram) jar black currants in vodka syrup, strained, liquid reserved
scant 1 cup heavy cream, chilled

Method

1. Cut the filo into 8 equal squares, using scissors. Take 4 muffin tins and place 2 filo squares in each, at right angles, so that 8 points stick up. Push the sheets down firmly to create cups.
2. Bake at 350°F for 20 to 30 minutes, until golden. Combine the butter and honey together and use this mixture to brush the pastry cups before returning them to the oven. Bake for 10 minutes more, then let cool.
3. Slightly crush some of the black currants. Whip the cream until stiff peaks form, then fold in the strained fruit and some of their syrup.
4. Spoon the fruit-cream fool into the filo cups with some syrup spooned over or around, as well, if desired. Eat immediately, while the textures and tastes are at their most pristine.

dried vegetables

Although less essential than in the past, dried vegetables are still a practical addition to any pantry, as long as you buy those with decent taste, texture, color, and aroma. Today's dried vegetables fall into two main categories: the "luxury exotics," which include sea vegetables (seaweeds), and the ultraconvenient soup mix or pasta sauce packs, which come ready-mixed. Essentially food that has been processed or pounded, these last two can be used to thicken sauces or add interest to pasta or rice, or they can be mixed with sea salt flakes and cracked pepper as a creative seasoning.

3 Mixed vegetables This mix is the basis of many inferior packet soup mixes worldwide. However, a good-quality, chunky, and aromatic mix, added to tomato, chicken, or mixed vegetable soups, can quickly boost flavor, color, and taste; allow time for full rehydration. Ground to a powder, the mix can thicken and enrich pasta sauces.

4 Vegetable crisps Reputable brands of vegetable crisps, which contain colorful vegetables such as blue potatoes, beets, and carrots, crushed, make a novel crispy topping on gratin dishes or baked fish. Or stir them into cream cheese with garlic as a dip.

5 Nori The best-known Japanese seaweed, nori is made from a red seaweed that is reduced to a pulp and then dried like paper. It is used as a wrap for sushi, but it can also be torn into bits or scissor-shredded, for use in cold noodle salads, or as a texture-color-taste booster for pasta dishes.

6 Wakame This fine, slightly pleated brown seaweed, which turns green in boiling liquids, has a delicate texture, and adds appeal to textural Asian dishes in which a mild sea salt tang is useful: for example, in prawn or squid dishes, and noodle or rice dishes. Dry, it can be ground to a powder and sprinkled into or over fine noodle dishes.

7 Arame These thin, brittle seaweed shreds are brilliant when added to seafood dishes at the start of cooking; they hydrate to wiry, chewy strands, with a salty-sweet taste. Added to rice, noodles, and even vegetable stews, casseroles, or soups, they provide contrast and body, as well as a taste of the sea.

8 Kombu (konbu) When rehydrated in boiling water or stock, this ribbonlike seaweed turns soft and chewy, and has an intense sea salt savor. It boosts fish stocks, seafood stews, and Japanese fish-rice dishes, and is essential for authentic sushi rice. If used in stir-fries, it must be fully presoaked first. Kombu can also be used as a flavorant that is removed (as for bouquet garni).

1 Sun-dried tomatoes When dried, tomatoes (technically fruits) are wonderfully meaty and sweet, with a sharp aftertaste. The leather-dry tomatoes sold in packets (as opposed to those packed in oil) are the most versatile. Rehydrate them in boiling stock, then slice them into pasta sauces or salads. Or whiz them up with garlic, olive oil, anchovies, and stock and use as a spread.

2 Arrabbiata capsicum mix This strong-flavored mix of dried chiles and sweet peppers (sometimes with milder additions, such as zucchini) is extremely useful. Rehydrated, it can be sprinkled into soups, or used in pasta or rice sauces to add sweetness, hotness, and color. Or use it with oil and lemon juice as an instant dressing or marinade.

squid, noodle, and seaweed salad

When rehydrated, dried seaweed has an alluring scent and taste of the sea, intriguing chewy texture, and curious colors. This salad makes the most of all these features, adding the sweetness of squid, chile, and garlic.

Serves 4–6

Ingredients
1 ounce dried wakame sheets
1 ounce dried arame strips
1 ounce dried hijiki shreds
4 ounces wide dried rice noodles
12 small fresh squid (about
    12 ounces)
1 tablespoon chile oil
2 teaspoons roasted sesame oil
1 tablespoon avocado oil
2 cloves garlic, chopped
½-inch chunk fresh ginger, peeled
    and grated
Juice of 1 lemon or lime
Sea salt, crushed, and freshly
    ground black pepper
1 tablespoon seaweed seasoning
    (optional)

Method
1. Put all the dried seaweed into a colander placed in a heatproof bowl. Pour enough near-boiling water over it to cover. Let soak for 5 to 8 minutes, until the seaweed is plump, fleshy, and softened. Lift out of the colander, leaving the liquid in the bowl, and rinse in cold water.

2. Add the rice noodles to the hot liquid in the bowl. Let soak until softened, then drain while still firm. Rinse the noodles in cold water and add them to the seaweed.

3. Prepare the squid: Trim off and keep the tentacles; discard the eye section, including the beak, empty the gut contents and discard the clear backbone or quill. Slice open the squid, and make score marks in a crisscross pattern on the skin side (outside) of half of them.

4. Heat the oils, garlic, and ginger in a large frying pan. Add the squid and stir-fry for 1 to 2 minutes, until opaque and tender. Toss in the drained seaweed and noodles, add the lemon juice and seasonings, and serve.

mushrooms

Not only does drying enable us to use a range of mushrooms that are unavailable fresh, but dried mushrooms are an extremely useful source of flavor and texture in everything from sauces to pasta and rice dishes. Certain mushrooms, such as porcini and morels, are outstanding when dried, meaty and intensely strong in flavor. Some, such as wood ear mushrooms, are prized mainly for their texture and appearance, while others, such as chanterelles, have a defined, if modest taste. Most dried mushrooms need soaking in hot water, but the resultant stock can often be used in the cooking.

Bottled and canned mushrooms retain their flavor less well than their dried counterparts, but are often pleasantly textural. Use onion, garlic, fresh herbs, spices, or Asian flavoring such as soy sauce to bring out the mushrooms' flavor.

dried mushrooms

1 Wood ear (Black fungus) The best Auricularia ("ear") mushrooms, often Chinese, are thin, tiny and black all over. When rehydrated, they magically balloon out and are silky and delicately chewy. Wood ears are good stir-fried or steamed, or added to Asian-style stews and noodle or rice dishes.

2 Fairy-ring mushrooms These tiny mushrooms are superb in clear soups and creamy sauces. Not as intensely flavored as many wild mushrooms, they suit quenelles, beignets, ravioli, and white poultry and fish mousses. Do not overwhelm them by using with boisterous wines.

3 Mixed mushrooms Dried mush-room mixtures often contain a poor mix of undistinguished fungi such as oyster and chestnut mushrooms. Look for "woodland mix" selections, including porcini, morels, and fairy-

ring mushrooms. Use in soups, sauces, stuffings for pancakes, ravioli, and omelets, and in casseroles and pasta sauces.

4 Chanterelles (girolles) Usually French or Italian, these delicious mushrooms range from small, pale, delicate specimens to dark-gilled large ones. Rehydrate them in hot broth or wine, and add garlic, herbs, and maybe Marsala, butter, olive oil, or cream for extra richness. They work beautifully in fricassees, soups, sauces, risottos, and pasta dishes.

5 Morels These prized black-capped fungi are almost better dried than fresh. Rehydrate them in hot stock or wine, and add butter or olive oil, garlic, and herbs: Use this as a base for a delicate soup or as a sauce for chicken breast, white

fish, pasta, risotto, or polenta. Ground to a powder, dried morels can season soups and risottos.

6 Porcini (*Boletus edulis***, or cèpes)** Of the various types of porcini, it is the classic French *Boletus edulis* that is the most prized. Look for unbroken slices, although smaller pieces are fine if all you want is flavor. Beware cultivated Asian porcini with no smell; the best are usually from France or Italy. Use them, rehydrated in white wine or stock, in soups and sauces for poultry, meat, vegetables, polenta, and pasta, or in risottos.

7 Shiitake These cultivated Asian fungi with speckled caps and inedible stalks rehydrate to plump vegetables with a pleasing chewy "bite" and slightly sulfurous taste. Use them, soaked, to add taste and texture to vegetable stir-fries and chicken stews, or to garnish clear, flavorful broths.

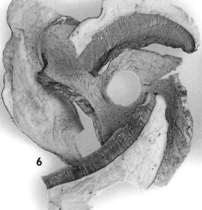

canned or bottled mushrooms

1 Porcini Bottled porcini, such as the Polish variety pictured, should be plump, brightly colored, and fairly intact. Heated gently, with olive oil, onion, and garlic, they are delicious served on toast. Or cook them, sliced, with cream, wine, and herbs as an appetizer, a side-dish, part of a sauce, or pureed in rich broth as a velvety soup.

2 Mixed wild mushrooms Bottled wild (or "forest") mushrooms should comprise a tasty assortment of fungi, such as porcini, morels, straw, and pied de mouton mushrooms. Sauté them in garlicky butter, goose fat, or olive oil, scatter with parsley, and then use them on toast, as a sauce for pasta or rice, or as part of a braised pork dish.

3 Straw mushrooms These Asian (usually Chinese) mushrooms are softly chewy and quite delicate. Drain off the preserving liquid (this is rarely well flavored) and heat the mushrooms in peanut oil, with ginger, garlic, and herbs, or add them to clear chicken or vegetable soups, stir-fries, or fine noodle or tofu dishes for texture and color. They also taste good combined with bamboo shoots, bean sprouts, and scallions in fritters or omelets.

4 Black truffles Bottled truffles may lack the glorious aroma and taste of the fresh variety, but they are still useful as long as you buy whole truffles. Use them sliced and heated (in truffle oil, chicken stock, wine, or other flavorful liquid), as a novel garnish for chicken breast or white fish fillets, or on poached or soft-boiled eggs. Or slice them and mash them up with garlic, lemon juice, salted butter, and parsley for steaks, chicken breasts, pasta, or grilled white fish.

5 Chanterelles (girolles) Often French or Italian, but found all over Europe, these delicious mushrooms can be delicately savory or strong in flavor. Heat them in butter, olive oil, duck or goose fat, with garlic and onions, add wine, rich stock, or cream (and a splash of Marsala, if desired), and use in rice or noodle dishes, soups, sauces, or soufflés, with chicken, veal, or lamb.

vegetables in oil, brine, or juice

Relatively few of us know the pleasure of strolling in the garden to pick a bundle of vine leaves or pluck a ripe red pepper straight from the plant. So we should celebrate the fact that such good, interesting vegetables are now available in bottles, cans, or packets. Add a squeeze of lemon, some sizzling, garlicky butter, vinaigrette or mayonnaise, and a delicious snack, salad, or meal may be just around the corner. And don't throw away the processing liquid without tasting it: When good, this can enhance soups, stews, glazes, sauces, and marinades. Always look for authentic products, with adequate information about their provenance and suggested uses.

1 Vine leaves Even when blanched and brined, grape vine leaves keep their perfect shape and texture. Often Greek or Turkish in origin, the leaves can be used to wrap all sorts of foods, including cooked or semicooked rice mixtures, minced cooked meats, and even fish balls. Cook or heat stuffed vine leaves through thoroughly in lemony stock, then drizzle them with extra-virgin olive oil.

2 Roasted sweet bell peppers Superbly succulent sweet peppers (or pimiento), from the Mediterranean, preserve beautifully after roasting; the sweet, oily syrup in which they are sold is often delicious too. In salads, they are the ultimate easy ingredient, even served with just olive oil and garlic. They are lovely in soups and purees, or sliced into pasta or rice. Or stuff them with salt cod puree, cheese mixtures, or garlicky potato.

3 Eggplant in oil Sliced, chargrilled eggplant packed in good olive oil or vinaigrette can be tasty, useful, and

time-saving. Use them in salads with tuna, capers, and olives, or with beans. Puree them with garlic, parsley, and hummus and use as a spread, or slice them into ribbons to mix with chile-hot satay dressing and serve on rice.

4 Cherry peppers These miniature, mildly hot capsicums usually come from Hungary, Spain, or South Africa. Packed in sweetish brine or oil, they stay pert, chewy, and colorful. They are best eaten whole, as an appetizer with salty white cheese, mixed with olives, or as part of a salad. Served with cured meats, they make an excellent brunch dish.

5 Artichoke hearts Because artichokes need extensive preparation, canned or bottled artichoke hearts are very convenient. They are available either whole or halved; beware of unlined cans, which can leave the artichokes with a metallic taste. Simply add lemony dressings or aioli, or mix the hearts with tuna and mayonnaise as a salad. Pureed in stock and cream

with tarragon, artichoke hearts can be transformed into a quick soup.

6 Passata This tasty, semithick puree of tomatoes is sold under many different names worldwide, usually in bottles or cartons. The best, often Mediterranean or American, can be delicious enough to drink straight and is always useful to keep on hand to add body, color, and sweetness to savory dishes. Use it in risotto, baked with pasta, or even, if well seasoned, as soup.

7 Plum tomatoes Though not comparable to fresh tomatoes, canned plum tomatoes add color and are very convenient. Use them in stews, bakes, soups, sauces, and blended drinks.

Usually made from Roma or other fleshy plum tomatoes, they come either chopped (a) or whole and peeled (b). Avoid those in brine—the tastiest come packed in juice. And avoid those with added herbs or spices: it's best to add your own seasonings.

8 Sweet corn kernels Preserved in light brine, sweet and mild sweet corn kernels (niblets) are a useful addition to many high-protein dishes, and salads. Puree them in a food processor with garlic, onion, butter, and paprika, and serve as mash, or blend them with stock, cream, bacon, chiles, and cooked potatoes for chowder.

9 Hearts of palm These young leaf shoots of certain types of palm tree are prized for their silky texture and delicacy. Use them in a salad with vinaigrettes or in ceviche. Wrap them in prosciutto or bacon and bake; slice them into rounds and stir-fry; or add them to rich poultry or meat dishes for color and texture.

10 Bamboo shoots These silky, delicate, mild-tasting Chinese vegetables are best bought whole rather than in slices. Drain and slice them into chunky diagonals or quarters to use in stir-fries, rice, or noodles, or halve them and add them to chicken stews. They work well in satay dishes, green or red Thai curries, and hot-sour dishes.

11 Water chestnuts These popular Chinese tubers, available peeled and whole in cans, are crisp and mildly sweet-tasting, and add pleasing texture and taste to stir-fries, noodle and rice dishes, fritters, pancakes, and spring rolls. More unusually, try them in a salad with scallions, chiles, and a garlicky sesame and rice wine dressing.

Water chestnuts can also add crunch to omelets, chicken stews, and pork dishes, especially with anise or Szechuan pepper seasonings.

wild mushroom, potato, and prosciutto gratin

In this dish from Paul Gayler, celebrated chef at London's Lanesborough Hotel, dried mushrooms are used to flavor a creamy gratin—"one of my favourite gratins, full of flavor and delicately creamy," says Paul. "The prosciutto could be replaced with smoked ham, which is equally delicious."

Serves 4

Ingredients

½ ounce dried morels
½ ounce dried porcini
2 tablespoons unsalted butter
2 shallots, finely chopped
1 clove garlic, crushed
2 ounces prosciutto, minced
1 teaspoon fresh thyme leaves
2 large waxy potatoes (about
    14 ounces), washed, unpeeled
2¾ cups heavy double cream
Salt, freshly ground black pepper,
    and nutmeg
1 tablespoon freshly grated
    Parmesan cheese

Method

1. Reconstitute the dried mushrooms in lukewarm water for 30 minutes, then drain well.
2. Heat the butter in a frying pan, add the mushrooms, and cook over high heat for 4 to 5 minutes; add the shallots, garlic, prosciutto, and thyme and cook for 2 to 3 minutes longer, then remove to a bowl.
3. Thinly slice the potatoes and place them in a large bowl. Bring the cream to a boil, then pour it over the potatoes, season with salt, pepper, and nutmeg to taste, and toss well.
4. Remove enough potatoes from the cream to make a single layer in the bottom of a well-buttered, shallow baking dish about 12 inches in diameter.
5. Sprinkle some of the mushroom mixture over, then top with more potatoes. Continue to layer until all the potatoes are used up. Pour any remaining cream over the layers just to cover. Scatter with a final layer of mushroom mixture and sprinkle with the cheese.
6. Bake in an oven preheated to 375°F, for about 1 hour, until the top is golden and bubbly, and the potatoes are cooked so that a slender knife can be easily inserted through all the layers. Remove from the oven and let stand for 5 minutes, then serve.

mackerel salad niçoise-style

Although far from the classic salade niçoise, this version is hugely appealing in its marriage of creamy smoked mackerel with the sharpness of the pickled and marinated vegetables. Additions such as parsley, red onion rings, and cucumber can be included at will.

Serves 4

Ingredients

2 fillets smoked mackerel (about 9 ounces)

12 crisp and curly lettuce leaves

2 hard-cooked eggs, peeled and quartered

24 green or black salt-cured olives (or a mixture)

5 ounces marinated globe artichoke hearts, quartered

4 tablespoons salted or pickled capers, rinsed

2 tablespoons pickled cornichons (gherkins), sliced

4 marinated sun-dried tomatoes, cut into strips

4 tablespoons extra-virgin olive oil

1 tablespoon cornichon pickling liquid or caper vinegar

Method

1. Flake the mackerel into chunky chevrons, discarding the skin. Set aside.

2. Tear up the lettuce and arrange it in the bottoms of individual salad bowls, followed by some egg quarters.

3. Scatter in the remaining solid ingredients, adding the fish last.

4. Whisk together the oil and the cornichon pickling liquid or vinegar.

5. Serve the salad chilled with the dressing drizzled over.

olives

The Mediterranean has long been the major source of most eating olives, but other countries, from Morocco to Mexico, have their own olive cultures. The name of a table olive variety, such as Nyons or Kalamata, generally defines its place of origin or the olive's particular characteristics, but precise definitions are tricky; many olives are sold simply as "green" (unripe) or "black" (ripe).

There is no right or wrong way when it comes to choosing olives: Buy those that you most enjoy. Bear in mind, however, that tiny olives suit pizza, for example, while fat, soft, squashy ones make great pastes and spreads. Almost all olives are good as appetizers, served with crusty bread and olive oil, with salami or prosciutto, or other appropriate foods.

Avoid unshiny, perfectly shaped black olives in a jet-black liquid: Such indifferent products are picked too early and "cured" using metallic reagents: not ideal. Whenever possible, taste olives before you buy them as they spoil very easily, even when shop-bought.

1 Kalamata olives Named after the area of Greece from which they come, Kalamata olives are glossy, firm, and salty. Stir them into tomato-based stews, bake them with whole fish, or add them to a classic Greek salad.

2 Nyons olives These tiny, chewy, black Provençal olives are used, most famously, to decorate pissaladière and pizza. They are delicious in ratatouille and in tuna and goat cheese salads, or just plain with crusty bread and olive oil.

3 Moroccan black olives These dryish, chewy olives, which you can buy in bitingly hot harissa marinade, go well with sardines and anchovies, and in vegetable tagines.

4 Italian green olives These large, fleshy olives taste clean and fresh and have a crunchy texture. Crush them lightly and marinate them in hot olive oil with coriander and fennel seeds, crushed garlic, and dried red chile flakes: delicious.

5 Oven-dried Provençal olives These soft, wrinkly olives are available either green or black (pictured), and are the true taste of Provence. Oven-dried, often salt-cured, and with Provençal herbs added, they have an intense, dry richness. Easily squeezed to remove the pits, these olives are perfect party food. Try them with pasta, in fish stuffings with fennel and lemon, or use them for tapenade.

6 Lucques olives These splendidly pert, angle-nosed green olives, often available in the south of France and North Africa, have a lean, dense, and meaty flesh. Add them to tomato and eggplant dishes, or use them in Moroccan-style salads, with orange, red onion, orange flower water, and cardamom, for example. Chopped, they make excellent green olive paste with lemon juice, garlic, and oil.

7 Greek Volos olives These plump, purplish olives come from the Greek mainland town of Volos and are often packed in fruity olive oil with peppercorns and oregano.

Less sharp than Kalamata olives, they are excellent all-purpose olives. Use them as part of a mezze. Easily crushed and pitted, they are good in purees or as a stuffing, with extra garlic and parsley, for rolled lamb.

8 Stuffed olives Spanish green olives, particularly firm and mildly salty Manzanilla olives, are some of the world's finest. Stuffed with tiny chiles (a), lemon zest (b), anchovy fillet pieces (c), or almonds (d), they make perfect tapas. Or use them in rice dishes, or in chicken, seafood, or pork stews.

preserved meat, game, poultry, & fish

sausages and salamis

The tradition of our ancestors to let nothing go to waste when a pig was butchered led to the creation of many delicious products, of which sausages and salamis are prime examples.

A mixture of lean and fat meat, dry-cured and chopped to various degrees of coarseness, and then stuffed into natural gut casings and matured, salamis come in innumerable variations. The best come from France, Italy, and Spain and take time and skill to make. Sadly, most imported salamis are industrial versions of the real thing. Just because a salami is called Milano doesn't mean that it comes from Milan. Beware luridly colored, overseasoned salamis that have artificial casings and a soapy taste. Pick expensive salamis, which are irregular in size or in the distribution of the lean and fat meat. A good deli is more likely to sell authentic salamis than a supermarket.

Good-quality salamis, often flavored with garlic, pepper, and spices, are delicious eaten as part of an antipasto, with gherkins, sun-dried tomatoes, or other accompaniments, but they can also be useful additions to salads and simple cooked dishes. Other sausages, such as cotechino and boudin blanc, are ready-cooked rather than cured, and just need reheating before eating.

1 Saucisson sec This French dry-cured pork sausage often comes in a loop shape, inside an edible gut casing that may have a layer of whitish bloom. It is dense, waxy, and mild, and may be smoked. It is eaten raw and thinly sliced, usually as part of an hors d'oeuvre. It also works well in a leafy salad, with black olives.

2 Salame Milano A mixture of pork and beef or veal, this mellow-tasting salami is often mass-produced. Cube it into potato or green salads, or serve it as part of a cold meats platter.

3 Salame Napoletano This classic spicy salami, made from either pure pork or a mix of pork and beef, contains hot red pepper, which gives it its characteristic hotness, sharpness, and balanced sweet taste. Use it on pizza, with roasted red peppers and anchovies, or to spice up a tomato, mozzarella, and basil salad.

4 Salame di Veneto This attractively dappled, deep red salami is mellow and sweetly aromatic. It makes superb sandwiches with arugula, black pepper, and olive oil.

5 Salame Felino Distinguished by its ties and slightly uneven, bulbous shape, this highly regarded Italian salami is flavored with peppercorns, garlic, and white wine. It is soft pink when cut and mild-tasting. Serve it, thinly sliced, with raw fennel and olives, drizzled with olive oil. Or team it with radicchio, red onions, caper-berries, and a spoonful of mascarpone.

6 Luganega This Italian uncooked, cured country pork sausage, flavored with coriander, pepper, and red wine, is also made in Greece, where it is known as *lukanika*. Sold coiled in vacuum packs, it can be grilled, broiled, or fried, and served, cut in pieces, as a mezze or antipasto. Removed from the casings, and cooked with garlic, olive oil, bay leaves, and wine, luganega makes a superb pasta sauce. Alternatively, serve it grilled whole, with sautéed potatoes.

7 Smoked boiling sausage This mild, soft-textured cooked sausage, often sold in a U shape or coiled, comes in many styles. If the sausage is truly smoked (and not simply "smoke flavored" with chemicals), it has a distinctive taste. German varieties tend to be denser, darker, and most flavorful, and are superb in soups, stews, and potato dishes.

8 Black pudding This blood sausage exists in various guises all over Europe: British black pudding, French, *boudin noir* and Spanish *butifarra* are the best-known versions. With additions such as pork fat, onions, and spices, it can taste superb. Already cooked, black pudding is easy to prepare: Slice and sauté it with bacon and eggs, or use it with bacon in white bean stews.

9 Boudin blanc Creamy-textured "white pudding" is made all over Europe, but French *boudin blanc* is particularly prized. Usually made of veal, pork, and chicken, sometimes of fish, *boudin blanc* may also be flavored with truffle (pictured). It is ready-cooked, so it simply needs reheating briefly: Poach or steam the sausage whole before slicing. Use it in bean or cabbage stews, in salads with bacon and egg, or in potato dishes.

10 Cotechino This famous plump and tender pork sausage from Italy is usually sold ready-cooked with seasoned lentils in a vacuum-packed bag: All it needs is reheating. Popular at Christmas and New Year, it can be eaten plain, drizzled with olive oil, or served cooked, but cold, as a salad, with vinaigrette.

11 Lap cheung These rough-textured sausages from China are mild, sweet, and spicy, and consist mainly of pork. Since they are only lightly cured, they should always be cooked thoroughly. If using whole, boil them for at least 10 minutes.

Or slice and steam, sauté, or stir-fry them before adding them to vegetable or chicken dishes. Use in rice and noodle dishes, in stir-fries, or minced in wraps or dumplings.

12 Chorizo This delicious, chewy, paprika-spiced pork sausage is made with smoked pork in Spain, and fresh pork in Mexico. It may be bought either cooked or uncooked. The ready-to-eat chorizo (a) is superb served with cheese and olives, or added to salads or piperade. The uncooked chorizo (b) can be cooked with beans, potatoes, or rice, or added to soups and salads, to add spice and color. When cooking or heating chorizo, the sausage oozes a gorgeous red, spicy oil, which can be used as a dressing.

13 Kabanos Coarsely cut, dense, and chewy, these cured (and often smoked) pork sausages from Poland are delicious sliced and added to omelets, soups, or casseroles, or to a beet and red onion salad.

7 8 11 12a 10 9 12b 13

storage

Store dried, cured, smoked, or other preserved sausages and salamis in a cool, dark, dry place, ideally unwrapped or in loose waxed paper wrappers. Most, once cut, should be refrigerated. Others keep well on cool pantry shelves. Always cut whole salamis at the time of use.

ham and bacon

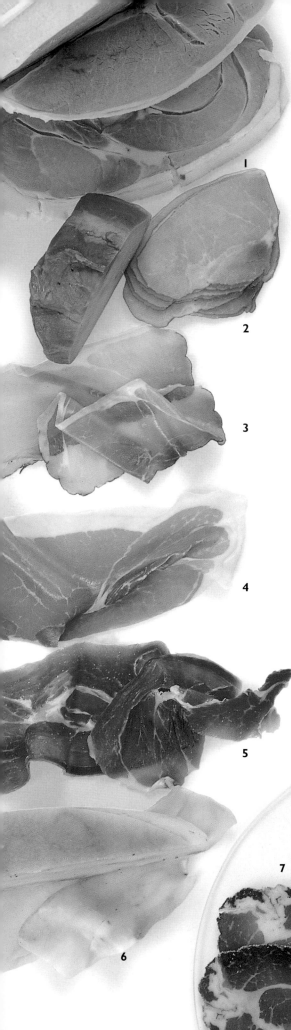

Ham and bacon are both cured pork: The ham is the hind leg, while bacon is from the loin or rib areas. The curing is either wet, where the meat is soaked in brine, or dry, where salt (or saltpeter) and seasonings are rubbed into the meat: This last method is the more traditional and slower, and is far superior.

Cured "raw" hams, such as Parma ham, are dry-cured and then air-dried, and tend to be silky and sweet, and are usually eaten thinly sliced. Hams that are cured and then cooked are paler, denser, and firmer, and mild in flavor. A dry or wet cure, the salts and sugars used in the cure, slow or quick maturation, the type of wood used for smoking—all these things affect the taste, look, texture, and usability of the final product.

1 York ham Dry-cured and then baked, York ham tastes sweet, mild, and salty. If bought sliced straight from the bone, it is most likely to have been traditionally cured. Slivers added to creamy pasta sauces, potato dishes, and omelets are delicious, and it also tastes great in scrambled eggs.

2 Kasseler Generally thought of as Polish, versions of this are made all over Europe, such as *lomo ahumado,* from Spain. Kasseler is lean meat pork loin that is cured and then smoked. Rosy pink and very tender, with hardly any visible fat, Kasseler is best sliced wafer-thin and eaten plain.

3 Black Forest ham This delicious, raw cured German ham is firm but tender, assertively smoky, and delicately sweet. It is delicious eaten alone or with warm potatoes.

4 Parma ham (prosciutto di Parma) The king among raw hams (*prosciutto crudo)*, made in and around Parma in Italy, is cured in salt, massaged, and hung for up to a year. Other Italian raw hams, such as Prosciutto di San Daniele, can be almost as good. Real Parma ham is too good to cook: Eat it straight, wrapped around asparagus, or draped over melon slices.

5 Serrano ham (jamón serrano) This fine, air-dried mountain ham is made in southwestern Spain, most famously in Jabugo. The unhurried curing process produces a deep, elegant flavor, rosy color, and sweetness. Try it with membrillo, olives, or slivers of goat cheese.

6 Lardo (speck, tocino)
Consisting almost entirely of fat, this creamy, dense, and flavorful salt-cured bacon is made in Italy (where it is known as *lardo*), Germany (*speck*), and Spain (*tocino*).

Often thinly sliced and eaten raw on coarse bread, it is also wonderful to cook with. When heated, it renders an aromatic fat that is superb for sautéing potatoes. It can also add moisture and flavor to minced meat mixtures.

7 Coppa This Italian cured collar of pork (the meat is pressed into sausage skins and then hung to dry and mature) is much fattier, and therefore cheaper, than *prosciutto crudo*. Delicious sliced wafer-thin and eaten as an antipasto, it also goes well in pasta sauces or polenta.

8 Pancetta This delicious Italian bacon, cured with herbs and spices, rolled, and pressed between boards that flatten it to a tight block or roll, is very occasionally sold smoked, but usually unsmoked.

Buy it in a piece and dice it or thinly slice it to use with spaghetti, garlic, and cream, or in tomato-caper sauces for pasta. Wrap thin slices of pancetta around chicken breast pieces, white fish, or oysters and bake until crisp.

9 Bacon The quality of bacon varies enormously, depending on whether it is factory- or farm-produced. The former is made by injecting brine into the meat, which speeds up production but means that lots of water is released into the pan as the bacon cooks; and the smoke flavor of factory-smoked bacon is usually synthetic. Farm bacon is more likely to be dry-cured, which produces a far superior flavor.

Fatty streaky bacon (a) can be sizzled in its own fat until crisp, and is fantastic added to pasta, gnocchi, potatoes, or rice. Back bacon (b) is a leaner product and is delicious fried, broiled, or baked. Serve it with sautéed apple rings; with chicken livers; with white or black pudding; or with waffles and maple syrup.

olive-studded pork loin with pancetta and bresaola

This elegant, lean pork roast, studded with almond-stuffed olives, has a wrap of smoked pancetta for salty moistness, bresaola for sweetness and color, and fresh rosemary for aroma and balance. A rocket salad and orzo pasta are good accompaniments.

Serves 4–6

Ingredients
1¼ pounds pork loin, boned, skinned, any visible fat removed
12 almond-stuffed green olives
Sea salt and freshly ground black pepper
2 cloves garlic, crushed to a paste
12 thin slices smoked pancetta (or smoked streaky bacon)
8 thin slices bresaola (cured beef)
1 sprig fresh rosemary
2 tablespoons extra-virgin olive oil
⅓ cup Pinot Noir or other robust red wine
½ tablespoon salted butter

Method
1. Blot the pork dry with using paper towel. Push a knife blade into the meat at regular intervals, and insert an olive into each hole. Rub the pork all over with the salt, pepper, and garlic.
2. Lay slices of pancetta so that they overlap along the length of the pork. Then wrap the bresaola slices around the roast to cover the meat.
3. Using kitchen string, tie the roast in 4 places. Push the rosemary sprig under the string. Set in a baking dish and drizzle with the oil.
4. Roast in an oven, preheated to 375°F, for 40 to 55 minutes, or until a meat thermometer inserted near the center registers 162°F. Remove the roast from the pan, cover it loosely with foil, and let it rest.
5. Place the roasting pan over high heat and pour in the wine, stirring to deglaze the pan. Add the butter and stir to mix until thickened.
6. Carve the meat into ½-inch-thick slices and serve it, hot or cold, with a drizzle of the sauce on top.

preserves and confits of meat, poultry, and game

Preserved and cured meats, like many gourmet foods, evolved out of necessity. But such is the desirability of the pronounced flavors, firmer textures, and appealing colors of these meats that we still produce them, even though a long shelf life is of less importance in our modern era. Even so, the fact that you can have a stock of canned or vac-packed meats in your larder or fridge means that a delectable meal is always near to hand. As well as making perfect uncooked appetizers, they can also add immense cachet to cooked main dishes.

Air- and smoke-drying, salting, sugar-curing, and the use of fats, spices, and herbs, along with precise and skillful treatment, ensure that these artisanal products remain tasty and convenient long after production. When buying, look for a clearly identifiable regional provenance, which should guarantee good and consistent quality and identity.

1 Pâté de campagne Good coarse "country pâté" is made of a balanced mix of lean and fat cooked meat, such as pork or game. Sealed with a layer of jelly or fat, terrines of pâté keep for weeks in a cool, dark place. Eat pâté straight with bread and coarse mustard, or use it in a salad with cooked potatoes.

2 Foie gras The finest of the many grades of fattened goose or duck liver is foie gras "entier" (or whole pieces), but foie gras "en bloc" is also excellent and cheaper: Liver pieces are marinated in sugar, salt, and port or Sauternes, and then cooked to a silken-smooth texture in cans or jars. (Avoid the foie gras parfaits or purees, which are padded out with other products.) Eat foie gras, chilled and sliced straight from the can, on toasted brioche. It can also make a superb steak butter.

3 Pork rillettes This rich, creamy French pâté is usually made from belly pork, which is poached gently in its own fat, shredded, and then returned to the fat and allowed to set firm. Rillettes from southwest France are superb. Eat it on hot toast, or spread it on ham, to roll up inside crusty rolls with gherkins.

4 Biltong A traditional southern African product valued for its long shelflife, biltong consists of narrow strips of game that are massaged to produce juiciness, rubbed in salt, and then sun-dried until leather dry; it may also be smoked. A snack food in its own right, biltong can also be used in cooking. Sliver it and drizzle with avocado oil as an antipasto, or grate it into sautéed potatoes.

5 Jerky Similar to biltong, jerky is meat that has been cut into strips and then sun- or fire-dried. It originated in Peru and became the classic trail food of the American west. Try grating or slicing it into cooked bean, potato, or pasta dishes.

6 Pastrami Lean, crimson pastrami, popular in the United States, is beef brisket or underside that has been dry-cured with salt, sugar, and spices, and then hot-smoked. Its dark edges and coarse texture make it easily identifiable. Serve it on rye bread, with mustard and dill pickles, or with coleslaw or sauerkraut.

7 Corned beef Also known as bully beef, canned corned beef is spicy, sweet, and fat-speckled. Highly nutritious and calorific, it was popularized as a wartime food. It can be sliced and eaten straight on bread with mustard or pickles, or torn into shreds and mashed into beans or potatoes.

8 Smoked venison This product, often from Scotland, is prepared from succulent lean venison, and is usually sold presliced in convenient vac-packs. It is best served cold, in sandwiches, with lettuce and red currant jelly, mustard, or even horseradish sauce.

9 Smoked duck breast Rosy or dark, with a delicious border of fat, smoked Muscovy duck breast is delicious served with chile jam and crisp lettuce, or with applesauce or red currant jelly as a sandwich. Alternatively, heat it briefly in meat stock and port, and serve with mashed beans and carrots.

10 Bresaola This northern Italian speciality (similar to Swiss Bündnerfleisch) is lean, prime beef that has been air-dried until fully matured. It keeps a superb dark red color, as well as its sweetness. Served sliced, drizzled with olive oil, and seasoned with a squeeze of lemon juice and a twist of black

3

5

4

7

8

9

6

10

11

pepper, it is the perfect antipasto.
Or wrap it around a pork roast.

11 Confit de canard Using an
ancient preservation method,
duck legs are cured (using sugar,
salt, and seasonings) and then
cooked slowly in their own fat
until very tender, usually in the
same vessel that they are sold in.
The fat sets solid as a seal, the
meat suspended between the fat
and the naturally developed
aspic below.

Add confit to cooked flageolet
beans for a quick cassoulet, or eat
it torn into shreds, with mustard.

12 Lacquered duck
Delicious, glossy, rich,
and flavorful, lacquered
duck is best bought
whole or halved from
an authentic Chinese
delicatessen or restaurant.
Prepared by air-drying and
curing in sugar, salt, and star
anise, it is coated many times
in an aromatic sticky glaze.
Eat it, shredded, with hoisin
sauce and crisp greens, wrapped
in a Chinese pancake, Peking
duck-style. Or chop it and add it
to vegetable or noodle soup, or to
quick-cooked wheat noodle dishes.

12

storage
Most of the products featured should be stored in a
cool larder, or the fridge. Refrigerate after opening, and use
within several days.

chorizo and butter bean stew with garlic and thyme

This recipe, from the renowned Cornish chef-restaurateur's cookbook *Rick Stein's Food Heroes*, is simplicity itself. It depends on large, plump butter beans (lima beans) and the spicy effects of good Spanish chorizo sausage. As Rick himself says "I've always felt that the most important point about cooking good food is getting the best produce in the first place." If time is short, substitute two large jars of Spanish butter beans (labeled "Judion de la Granja") instead of the dried type, adding them, drained, in Step 3.

Serves 4

Ingredients
2 cups dried Judion butter beans, soaked overnight
8 ounces hot chorizo for cooking, such as parrilla chorizo picante
3½ tablespoons olive oil
5 cloves garlic, thinly sliced
½ medium onion, finely chopped
¾ cup red wine
14 ounces canned chopped tomatoes
1 tablespoon fresh thyme leaves
½ teaspoon salt
2 tablespoons chopped fresh flat-leaf parsley

Method
1. Put the butter beans in a large pan with lots of water, bring to a boil and simmer for 1 hour, or until tender. Drain and set aside.
2. Cut the chorizo into thin slices. Heat the oil and garlic in a pan over a medium-high heat until the garlic begins to sizzle. Add the chorizo and cook until the slices are lightly browned on either side, then add the onion and continue to cook until it has softened.
3. Pour in the wine and cook until it has reduced to almost nothing. Add the tomatoes, thyme, butter beans, and salt, and simmer for 15 minutes.
4. Scatter the parsley over, spoon the stew into deep, warmed bowls, and serve with fresh crusty bread.

choucroûte

For this hearty Alsace dish, you can use all kinds of ready-cooked pork products, from black pudding to kasseler.

Serves 4–6

Ingredients
8 small waxy potatoes, peeled
1 small onion, thinly sliced
1¼ cups fragrant white wine (Riesling)
2¼ pounds prepared sauerkraut
2 tablespoons caraway seeds
1 tablespoon juniper berries, crushed
4½ to 5½ pounds assorted cured pork,
   ham, or bacon, or sausage chunks

Method
1. Put the potatoes, onion, and half of the wine into a large flameproof casserole and cook over medium heat for 10 minutes. Add the sauerkraut, caraway seeds, and juniper berries, and then tuck in the meats. Pour in the remaining wine.
2. Cover and simmer for 20 minutes, then uncover and raise the heat. Check that the meats are heated through, and cut them into smaller pieces so that there is a portion of each per serving. Return them to the pan and cook for 5 more minutes.
3. Serve the choucroûte in a large dish with rye bread and chilled Riesling.

duck confit with cannellini beans

One of the simplest and tastiest recipes ever, in which the beans balance the richness of the duck confit.

Serves 3–4

Ingredients
1 (1.5 kilo) jar or can duck confit
2 cloves garlic, crushed
½ to 1 teapoon sea salt, crushed
20 black peppercorns,
   crushed
2¼ pounds
   canned or bottled
   cannellini beans
Chopped parsley

Method
1. Stand the jar or can of confit in hot water for 5 minutes, and then gently ease out the contents.
2. Cut the duck confit into 3 or 4 equal portions and sizzle, skin down, in a dry pan over medium-high heat for 5 minutes.
3. Measure about ⅔ cup of the fat and all the jelly from the confit jar into a large flameproof casserole. Add the garlic, salt, and peppercorns, and then the duck meat.
4. Drain off and reserve the liquid from the beans, and tip them into the pan. Cover and cook over medium heat for 10 to 15 minutes. Pour in enough of the bean liquid to make a runny sauce. Turn up the heat until the stew bubbles hard.
5. Mash some of the beans in the pan to a rough puree.
6. Serve each chunk of confit with some of the bean mixture and scatter with some parsley. Eat with really good bread and a robust red wine.

fish and seafood in cans and jars

Sardines lined up on garlicky toast, Matjes herrings in a warm potato salad, exotic smoked sturgeon in a crisp pastry case, and unctuous anchoiade: These are just a few of the earthy pleasures that await us once we investigate the intriguing selection of fish and seafood preserved in cans and jars. Not only are these foods ready to eat, they are also easy to use, they're intensely flavorful, and have a long shelf life. Pay good money for canned seafood, which is only as good as the seafood that went into the can. Look for products preserved in oil, ideally good olive oil, rather than nasty sauces or marinades, which are often used to hide the lack of flavor of poor-quality fish or shellfish.

6 Snails These meaty creatures are often sold canned, with their shells in an adjacent pack. The large Burgundy snail and the smaller *petit-gris* are the best-known species. Ready-prepared for quick reheating, they are best baked in a "snail butter" of garlic, butter, parsley, tarragon, onions, and sometimes Pernod. Alternatively, reheat them in a garlicky red wine sauce.

7 Pickled herring (rollmops) Boneless, double herring fillets, rolled up in a vinegary marinade that sets the flesh dense and white, are known as rollmops. Use them in sandwiches, with beets, onion, or apple, or sliver them and toss with white cabbage, onion, currants, and mustard-dill dressing as a salad.

8 Matjes herrings in oil These lightly salted, marinated herring fillets are nutritious and tasty, and a Jewish favourite. Traditionally served with steamed potatoes, gherkins, and sour cream, they also taste good straight. Or cut the fillets into chunks and toss them with soft-cooked eggs, chives, and thinned mayonnaise to eat with bread.

4 Prawns Large, plump king prawn tails keep good color, texture, and flavor when brined and canned; the best ones often come from Scandinavia. The prawns are superb on toast with lemon mayonnaise and a sprinkle of chives and dill, and are useful in salads, too. Use both the liquid and the prawns in spicy seafood pilaus, fish soups, or creamy prawn curries.

5 Clams These sweet, nutty, and delicate bivalves are best canned in their shells. Use them in fish soup, with butter, garlic, onion, and white fish, or in a sauce for spaghetti or rice: Cook the liquid until its reduced to one-quarter of its volume, add onion, garlic, and olive oil or cream, return the clams to the sauce and reheat. Or eat them straight, with sizzled pancetta, lemon juice and parsley.

1 Smoked mussels Shelled mussels, hot-smoked to tenderness and sold packed in olive oil, are great eaten straight, or in rye bread sandwiches with onion and mayonnaise. Mashed together with butter, lemon juice, garlic, and parsley, they make simple rillettes, and they excel in fritters, pancakes, and salads.

2 Smoked oysters Salted and smoked oysters are intensely sea-flavored and delicious. Drain, add lemon juice, and eat them plain or on cream cheese–covered toast or garlicky bruschetta with red onion and basil. Or wrap them in pancetta and broil them; add them to a rice salad, or mash them to a paste together with lemon juice, garlic, cayenne, and mascarpone.

3 Crab The best canned crab is white, dense, and meaty. Fold the crabmeat into homemade mayonnaise, to be eaten with lemon juice and brown bread, or use it to stuff eggs; or toss the crab in a garlicky vinaigrette and pile it onto lettuce. The canning liquid is good in sauces and soups.

11 Mackerel en escabeche Fillets of horse mackerel, often Spanish, are canned using a hot, tomato-flavored marinade that effectively "cooks" the fish into dense flakes. Coarsely mashed, with butter, a little of the marinade, and parsley, it makes good rillettes, and it is also good in fish cakes or fish pie.

12 Tuna Various species of tuna are used for canning. The best, such as atún blanco, or white tuna (a), from Spain, has a satisfyingly meaty texture, and is relatively expensive. Yellowfin tuna (b), often Spanish, has a lighter meat and is also good quality. Always buy large steaks, packed in good olive oil, rather than fragments.

Flake tuna into salads or into fillings for pita, pancakes, or rolls, or puree it for sauces (tuna suits olive- and tomato-based sauces). Tuna is also excellent with mayonnaise and vinaigrette, and capers, gherkins, garlic, herbs, and lemon are all natural allies.

13 Sprats These small fish from the herring family, silvery gold from their hot dry-smoking, are delicious, but not widely available. Broil them briefly to serve with mustard or tomatoes on toast; add them to salads, or use them on pizzas instead of anchovies. Mashed together with lemon juice, butter, and cayenne, they make a quick pâté.

14 Smoked sturgeon Not commonly available fresh, sturgeon is deliciously meaty when smoked. Dryish and easily flaked, it is good as a salad, in a lemony mayonnaise or a yogurty vinaigrette. Pureed, with butter, garlic, and Pernod, it makes a good spread for toast.

9 Anchovies These small silver fish are valued as a food and condiment, particularly in Spain and Italy, where the best anchovies come from. They come salted and then canned, ideally, in olive oil (a), dry-salted (b), or marinated (c). Dry-salted and canned anchovies are the most useful, for boosting sauces, dressings, pastes, and butters, and for enriching meat dishes. Marinated anchovies should be eaten raw: Add them to salade Niçoise, or serve them as part of a stylish appetizer.

10 Sardines Young pilchards, sardines are a humble but hugely successful canned fish. The best are from Spain, Portugal, and France. Buy them whole and preserved in oil rather than in a marinade or sauce. Mashed together with butter, vinegar, and mace, they are great on toast. Layered with apple, onion, and cooked potato slices, they make a good main dish.

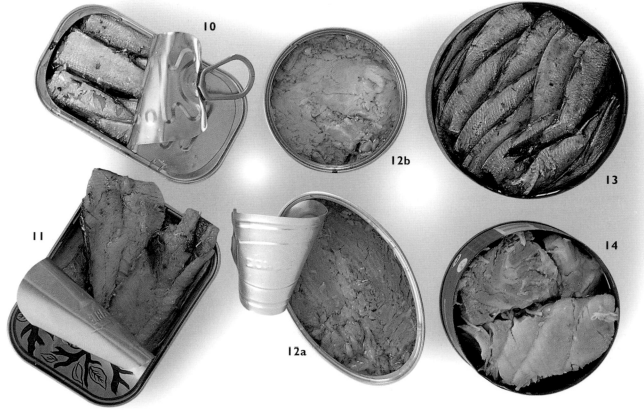

spaghetti with anchovy, tuna, and caper sauce

This delicious recipe is pantry cooking at its easiest and best.
If the basics are of good quality, the result can be spectacularly delicious.

Serves 4

Ingredients

12 ounces dried spaghetti
2 tablespoons virgin olive oil
2 cloves garlic, slivered
6 to 8 anchovy fillets in oil, drained
9 ounces (1½ cans) canned white
   tuna in olive oil, drained
3½ tablespoons white wine
6 tablespoons capers, rinsed and
   drained
3 tomatoes, chopped
4 sun-dried tomatoes in oil,
   chopped
16 basil leaves
2 tablespoons extra-virgin olive oil
Sea salt and freshly ground black
   pepper

Method

1. Cook the spaghetti in a large pot of boiling salted water for about 8 minutes or following the instructions on the box, until *al dente*.
2. Meanwhile, heat the 2 tablespoons virgin olive oil in a frying pan, and add the garlic. Sauté gently for 2 to 3 minutes.
3. Add the anchovy fillets and cook very gently until they break up and turn to a mush. Increase the heat and stir in the tuna.
4. Heat the fish mixture for a few minutes, covered, then pour in the wine and allow it to evaporate off and reduce. Stir in the capers, tomatoes, and sun-dried tomatoes.
5. Drain the pasta, reserving a little of the cooking water. Toss the spaghetti and the sauce together in a warmed serving bowl. Add a little of the cooking water if the sauce is too thick.
6. Stir in the basil and the 2 tablespoons extra-virgin olive oil and season with salt and pepper to taste. Serve hot, with some crusty bread and a lively white or red wine.

salt cod with chiles and garlic

This superb Basque dish is by American author and food expert Paula Wolfert, from her classic book *The Cooking of South West France*. In it, salt cod is simmered in garlic and olive oil until a rich, gelatinous emulsion forms. Chunky pieces of salt cod are best for this dish: You may have to buy more than you need, but you can use the off-cuts for brandade or for use with a garlicky aioli dip.

Serves 4

Ingredients

About 1 pound boneless salt cod
1 cup milk
4 tablespoons olive oil
4 cloves garlic, peeled and thinly sliced
1 small hot chile, cut into very thin strips
2 tablespoons chopped fresh parsley

Method

1. Soak the cod in cold water for 18 to 24 hours, changing the water three times, and adding the milk during the last soaking.
2. Rinse the fish. Cut into 8 equal chunks. Remove the bones and scales but not the skin (which is needed for its enriching gelatinous quality). Set each piece on waxed paper, on a plate. Chill in the refrigerator for about 20 minutes.
3. Place the salt cod chunks, skin side down, in a 10-inch round earthenware baking dish or an enameled cast-iron pan. Pour the oil over the fish and add the garlic. Put the dish over a low heat (a heat diffuser or trivet can prevent the dish from cracking).
4. Cook for 30 minutes, shaking the dish often so that the juices mix with the oil. Do not turn the fish, but shake and reposition the pieces to prevent sticking. Now and then, tilt the pan and spoon the simmering juices over the fish.
5. Near to serving time, increase the heat, and bring almost to boiling. Add the chile and parsley; cook to reduce the emulsifying juices somewhat, swirling constantly to combine the flavors. The result should be a smooth, blended sauce.
6. Serve hot, straight from the dish, or on individual serving dishes.

caviar and fish roe

All fish produce eggs (roe), but it is the many species of female sturgeon that produce the most valuable kind. The scarcity of sturgeon, and the precise skills required to turn the roe into caviar, mean that beluga, sevruga, and other caviars are an expensive luxury. Always buy caviar from a named producer, preferably Iranian, and look for eggs that are glossy, perfect, and separate (except for pressed caviar). Caviar can be used as a garnish—whether it's for lobster, scrambled eggs, sushi, or tagliatelle—but for most people it is best eaten plain, either alone or with soft-cooked egg, warm buckwheat blini, or thin hot toast.

1 Lumpfish roe The eggs of the North Atlantic lumpfish come dyed either red (a) or black (b). They add color and crunch to egg sandwiches, fish salads, and savory pastries, but are not good enough to be eaten on their own. Their cheapness and availability are the main appeal.

2 Beluga caviar The biggest eggs of all, from the biggest sturgeon of all, have a fine skin and delectable sea-fresh taste; they range in color from light gray to silvery black. Beluga XXL (pictured) is very rare, very large, and very expensive.

3 Sevruga caviar The sevruga produces fine-grained eggs, which are salty-sweet, intense in flavor, and less expensive than beluga. Classic Gray (pictured) is from a mature sevruga.

4 Oscietre caviar (osetra caviar) The oscietre sturgeon produces the widest range of eggs, the color varying according to the age of the fish. Medium-sized and delicately salty, they have superb mouth feel. Oscietre Gold (a) is from a younger sturgeon, and Oscietre Royal Black (b) is from an older one. Prized Imperial XO caviar (c) comes from an oscietre that is over 60 years old.

5 Tarama paste This pale gold or pink soft-cured cod's roe is the basis of most Greek taramasalata, made by mixing tarama, dampened bread crumbs, lemon juice, and olive oil.

6 Cod roe (in the piece) Salt-cured, sometimes smoked, this whole or partial lobe of cod roe is dense, ranging from spreadable to slightly crumbly; both the eggs and the skin can be eaten. Eat it sliced thinly, with lemon juice and/or olive oil, or mash it up with cream cheese, chives, and lemon juice.

7 Botargo This whole lobe of salted and dried mullet roe is encased in wax. Slice it thinly, discard the waxy rind, and drizzle with olive oil and/or lemon juice to eat alone. Or grate it (rind removed) over pasta or rice.

8 Pressed caviar Dense and sticky, pressed caviar is made from mixed caviar batches or immature and overripe eggs. Cheaper than other caviar, it tastes very salty, intense, and fishy, and is loved by many experts. Try it on hot toast, pancakes, or new potatoes.

9 Salmon roe (keta) These large cured salmon eggs have an intense salmon taste and pop pleasantly in the mouth. They cost much less than real caviar and can be used generously as a garnish for fresh or smoked salmon, and in sushi and sashimi.

10 Trout roe Orange-tinted, these cured sea trout eggs closely resemble salmon roe, but have a trout flavor and a finer mouth feel. Use on trout ceviche, mousse, rillettes, or pâté, or just on hot toast.

storage
Fresh caviar tastes incomparably better than pasteurized versions, and has a surprisingly long shelf life: up to three months if kept below 39°F. Once opened, refrigerate and eat within a couple of weeks.

cured fish and seafood

Smoking and drying are the most popular methods of preserving fish and seafood, usually after initial curing in salt. Smoking produces the greatest nuances of flavor, depending partly on the type of wood used. Cold smoking involves smoking the fish over a cool fire, so that the fish stays raw but becomes smoke-flavored, while hot smoking is done at a higher temperature until the flesh of the fish is cooked as well as flavored. Look for artisanal products, from a named source, and minimal ingredients: Salt and fish are all that is usually required.

1 Smoked salmon The best smoked salmon, cured with salt and then cold smoked, is worlds away from the cheaper products whose "smoked" flavor is injected in. High-quality smoked salmon should be eaten raw, or added to pasta or risotto at the last minute. Use farmed salmon in cooked dishes.

2 Kipper Herrings that have been split, salted, and then cold smoked, kippers are cooked, traditionally, by "jugging" (in a container of boiling water). Slices of kipper can be tossed with lime juice and chile for "ceviche," or used in kedgeree or pâté.

3 Smoked eel Look for rosy, striped eel in long pieces, which may come presliced. Use it as for smoked salmon. It goes particularly well with horseradish sauce, with dill, potato salad, and also bacon.

4 Salt cod (bacalau) Crucial to Iberian cuisine, salt cod must be well soaked in three changes of water for 24 hours before cooking. Use it for brandade (potato-fish puree) and in fritters, fish cakes, and fish stews. Stockfish, popular in Scandinavia, is similar, but is air-dried rather than salted.

5 Dried shrimp Intensely sweet-salty, these pretty, dried crustacea feature in many Asian dishes. Pounded or ground to a powder with spices, they can be sprinkled over food as a seasoning. Rehydrate them in fish stews, soups, and curries, or add them plain to rice, fritters, and omelets.

6 Bonito shavings (katsuobushi) These papery fine, pink Japanese bonito flakes have been shaved from a block of specially treated tuna. Use them as the basis of dashi stock, or dry as a garnish for marinated tofu or as a condiment.

7 Ikan billis These tiny, whole silver fish, preserved by curing in sugar and/or salt and then drying until crisp, are important in Asian cooking. Scatter them on rice or noodle dishes, shrimp curries, or stir-fried vegetables before serving.

8 Smoked mackerel Hot-smoked mackerel is useful and inexpensive. Flake or mash the tender flesh to use in salads with horseradish or mustard sauces, or mix with cream cheese, lemon juice, cayenne, and black pepper for a quick pâté.

9 Smoked trout Serve rosy and mild trout fillets with lemon juice and horseradish sauce, or mix with sour cream and dill as a topping for toast. Shredded and mixed with mascarpone, onion, paprika, and Tabasco sauce, it makes simple but tasty rillettes.

smoked salmon pizza

This pizza, invented by Wolfgang Puck, an influential chef-restaurateur and launcher of new trends in Californian cuisine, is lifted into the realms of luxury by the addition of smoked salmon.

Serves 2
(dough makes 4 x 8-inch pizzas,
topping covers 2 pizzas)

Ingredients

1 packet active dry yeast or
⅟₂ sachet fast-acting
(micronized) yeast
1 teaspoon clear honey
3 cups all-purpose flour
1 teaspoon kosher or rock salt
1 tablespoon extra-virgin olive oil
2 tablespoons chile and garlic oil
½ cup thinly sliced red onion
4 tablespoons dill cream (see
below)
5 ounces thinly sliced smoked
salmon
2 teaspoons chopped fresh chives
2 tablespoons sevruga caviar
(optional)

Method

1. To make the dough, combine the yeast, honey, and ¼ cup warm water in a bowl. In a mixer or food processor bowl, combine the flour and salt. Add the oil, the yeast mix, and ¾ cup more warm water.
2. Mix on a low speed, or pulse, in bursts, until the mixture comes away from the sides of the bowl. Turn the dough out and knead for 2 to 5 minutes. Cover with plastic wrap and leave to rise in a warm place for 30 minutes. When it is ready, it will stretch when pulled.
3. Divide the dough into two; one half will keep for 2 days in the fridge or can be frozen. Divide the remaining dough into 2 balls. Shape each by pinching the sides underneath, curving the top surface. Do this several times. Then roll the dough under your palm repeatedly for about 1 minute until smooth, and firm. Rest it for 15 to 20 minutes.
4. Place 2 pizza stones or heavy metal baking sheets in an oven, pre-heated to 475°F. On a lightly floured surface, stretch or roll out each piece of dough into a 8-inch circle, making the outer edge a little thicker than the center. Brush the dough with the oil and arrange the onion on top. Bake until the crusts are golden brown, 6 to 8 minutes.
5. Remove the crusts from the oven and set them on a firm surface. Spread the dill cream over the inner part of each and arrange slices of salmon to cover the pizzas. Sprinkle with chives. If you like, spoon a little caviar on top and serve immediately.

to make dill cream

Mix ¾ cup sour cream with 1½ tablespoons minced shallots, 1 tablespoon chopped fresh dill, 2½ teaspoons fresh lemon juice, and ⅛ teaspoon freshly ground white pepper. Mix well, refrigerate, and use as needed. The dill cream should keep well for up to 1 week.

oils, fats, & milk products

1   2   3   4   5   6

oils

In cooking terminology, oils are fats, derived from various plant sources, that are liquid at room temperature. Many of the oils on supermarket shelves are highly processed and often lacking in flavor. The best oils, obtained simply, without heat, such as cold-pressed extra-virgin avocado oil, stay deliciously true to their origins. Over twice as calorific as proteins and carbohydrates, oils should be used with restraint. High in monounsaturated fatty acids, olive oil is the most healthful oil to use in large quantities, while most other common oils are high in polyunsaturated fat and are best used in moderation.

Some oils, such as argan and pumpkin seed oil, are pungent, while sunflower and grapeseed oil are bland. Nuts or seeds may be roasted prior to the extraction of oil, which produces a darker color and stronger flavor. Flavored oils, such as chile or annatto oil, are useful, colorful and tasty, but aromatized or herb-infused oils spoil quickly. Avoid anything labeled simply "vegetable oil": Good oils always designate their type and origins.

Oils must be stored in a cool, dark, and dry place. Light and heat damage the molecular structure and will turn the oil rancid.

1 Sunflower oil This bland but nutritious oil is a workhorse oil for all purposes, and is not used for its taste. Use it in cakes, cookies and breads, braised dishes and stir-fries, or for deep-frying and sautéing.

2 Peanut oil The peanut contains about 50 percent oil and is a good source of vitamin E. The oil has a distinctive taste, especially when the nuts have been roasted. This is an all-purpose oil, but it suits African and Asian dishes, and spicy food.

3 Grapeseed oil Pressed from the seeds left behind after wine making, grapeseed oil is a light oil that is pleasant in most cooking, including in cakes. It works well in salad dressings and mayonnaise, and is also excellent mixed with an equal amount of extra-virgin olive oil.

4 Pumpkin seed oil This oil, which has long been popular in central and eastern Europe, has a wonderful, nutty flavor. Its color varies from yellow to dark brown depending on whether the pumpkin seeds were roasted before pressing.

7   8   9   10   11   12

Drizzle it over white cheese salads, or on pasta, gnocchi, poached meats, and vegetable purees.

5 Chile oil The vivid red color of this hot, chile-flavored oil is sometimes enhanced by food coloring. In Canton, it is used as a condiment in small side dishes. You can use it in Asian and Mexican cooking, for drizzling over fish, for example. Or try swirling it into toasted sesame oil with sea salt as a dip for crisp baby vegetables.

6 Sesame seed oil This is pressed either from unroasted seeds, which produces a fairly mild and pale oil, or from roasted seeds, which produces an oil as dark as mahogany, with a rich, intense flavor. Sesame oil benefits Chinese and Indian dishes, often being added in small quantities at the end of cooking, or used as a condiment.

7 Hazelnut oil Hazelnut oil may be pressed either from unroasted or roasted nuts. It is rich in vitamin E, distinctively nutty, and expensive. Use it as a condiment to add

nuttiness to cooked vegetables, chicken, fish, and dressings. For sautéing, combine one part hazelnut oil with two parts avocado or peanut oil.

8 Walnut oil Produced mainly in France and Italy, walnut oil is expensive and can have a very strong taste that does not appeal to everyone. Use it in tiny amounts as a condiment with chicken and steamed greens, or in nut pastes, bean purees, and vinaigrettes.

9 Palm oil (dende oil) An orange red oil, often semisolidified if cold, palm oil is produced from the fibrous fruit of the African oil palm. (Oil is also pressed from the inner kernels, but this is pale and more delicate.) It gives color and characteristic earthiness to African dishes. Use it in peanutty stews, chicken sautés, fish curries, and in pie fillings, but be warned that it is an acquired taste.

10 Mustard oil This yellow, spicy, pungent oil gives an intense hotness to dishes and is important in India

and other parts of Asia. Note, however, that this oil contains erucic acid and is considered by some authorities to be toxic. If you choose to try it, use it in minimal amounts as a condiment, or for tempering spices for fish dishes.

11 Avocado oil Developed in New Zealand for culinary use, avocado oil is an excellent source of vitamin E. Look for the cold-pressed extra-virgin variety, though it can be hard to find any version at all.
 Avocado oil's high smoke point makes it good for frying, but it is most often used as a condiment: Its greenish tones and fruity taste make it excellent with seafood, chicken, and mozzarella, and also in stir-fries.

12 Moroccan argan oil Produced from the fruit of the Moroccan ironwood tree (which is similar to the olive tree but unrelated), this is the latest in gourmet oil discoveries, and therefore expensive. Use it in tagines and couscous, or with stuffed flatbreads and goat cheese: It is distinctively pungent.

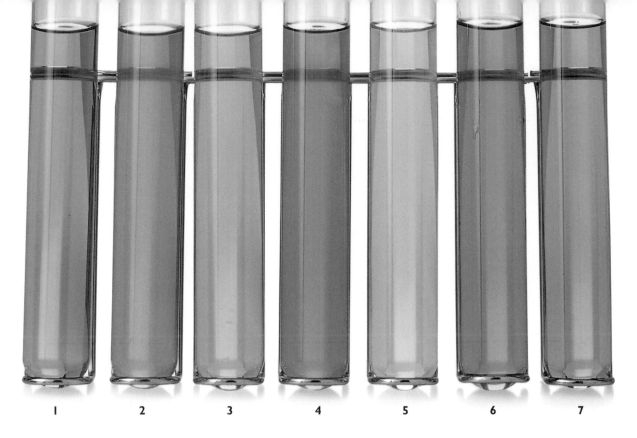

1	2	3	4	5	6	7

olive oil

Almost a pure fruit juice, olive oil is what is left once the olives have been pressed and the watery liquids removed. The best, least processed, olive oils retain all the fruits' natural antioxidants and vitamins, and have the best flavor.

Olive oil, produced mainly around the Mediterranean, is graded according to international standards. The different grades reflect, among other things, the degree of free acidity: The lower the free acidity, the smoother the taste. International brands often favor blends of different oils, since this ensures greater consistency from year to year. When buying the best extra-virgin olive oils, look for the country (or estate) of origin, the olive type, and the date and style of pressing. Be critical of the smell and taste: Buy only those that you enjoy. In Italy, northern oils made from early-picked olives have greater pepperiness than southern oils made from late-picked olives.

1 Affiorato (flor de aceite) This superb "flower of the oil" is as good as olive oil gets. Produced by crushing, before the main pressing begins, this free-run oil collects by gravity. It is made in France, Spain, Italy, Greece, and even in New Zealand, but is very rare and therefore expensive. Use it as a condiment, drizzled over salads, or with garlic and salt on crusty bread.

2 First cold-pressed, extra-virgin This prime and expensive product, which is obtained from the very first pressing, retains all the natural goodness of the olives, and has superb taste and smell.

Use it as for affiorato, for salads, dressings, or bread-dipping, and some low-temperature cooking.

3 Extra-virgin (supermarket grade) What's missing in this extra-virgin oil—"first" and "cold-pressed"—is

important, but many supermarkets commission consistent blends, which have a good color, smell, and taste, with no aggressive pepperiness and a fresh, fruity flavor. Perfect for everyday cooking, this oil can be used in all kinds of dishes: to sauté, pan fry, braise, stew, roast, or to use in soups, mayonnaise, vinaigrettes, and marinades.

4 Unfiltered extra-virgin Left unfiltered, extra-virgin olive oil is cloudy and dense but tastes delicious. Olive oil that is lightly filtered (using cotton wool in a funnel) also tastes superb. Use either unfiltered or lightly filtered olive oil where full flavor counts: on bread, grilled vegetables, poultry, fish, pasta, rice, or salads.

5 Virgin Obtained by one of the certified acceptable international

methods of production, virgin olive oil is the second-best grade after extra-virgin. While it may still have a respectable taste, this oil is best used for bulk cooking, deep-frying, or mass consumption.

6 Feral Another rare and curious olive oil, this prime, usually blended, product from hand-harvested, wild (feral) trees, has unique appeal and earthiness. Use it as a condiment, for dipping bread into, or for pouring over cooked fish or meat, or steamed vegetables.

7 Truffle-flavored Sold in tiny bottles, this expensive oil is made from extra-virgin olive oil that has been flavored with the aroma and taste of truffles: the best also contains truffle pieces, musky and sulfurous. Use truffle oil late in cooking, with pasta, rice, mushrooms, game, and foie gras.

using oil

Always match the oil to the style or origin of the dish. Oils with high smoke points, such as sunflower, peanut, and corn oils, are best for deep-frying. Virgin (but not extra-virgin) olive oil is also a useful frying medium. Oil that has been heated over and again in a deep fryer will become rancid—it will keep for longer if it is strained between frying and kept in a cool, dark place.

Vinaigrette

Put 1 tablespoon Dijon mustard in a jar or bowl. Add salt and pepper, some crushed garlic, and 2 tablespoons tarragon vinegar, cider vinegar, or red wine vinegar. Shake or whisk well. Add 6, 8, or 10 tablespoons extra-virgin olive oil (that is, 3, 4, or 5 times the volume of the vinegar), according to your taste. Shake or whisk again until a dense, yellow emulsion forms.

Use this as a salad dressing, a sauce for vegetables or tomatoes, or as an accompaniment for steamed or baked fish, eggs, or boiled meats. Store airtight, in a cool, dark place. Use within 2 weeks.

Note: Vinaigrette may separate: Simply shake or whisk it, and magically it will emulsify once more.

Herb tempura

Wash and pat dry 16 to 20 bouncy sprigs flat-leaf parsley or wild arugula. Whisk together 1 egg yolk, 1 tablespoon water, and 8 tablespoons fine rice flour. In another bowl, whisk 1 egg white together with a pinch of salt until frothy. Gently fold the two egg mixtures together.

In a medium pan, heat 2 inches of peanut oil, virgin avocado oil, virgin olive oil, or a mixture of these to about 360°F, until a ½-inch cube of bread browns in 30 seconds. Dip the herbs in the egg batter. Lower 3 or 4 sprigs gently into the hot oil and cook until pale, crisp, and golden: just 1 to 2 minutes. Drain them on crumpled paper towels. Serve hot, as snacks, with a dipping sauce such as tamari or sweet chile sauce.

 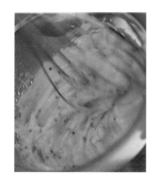

Mayonnaise

Put 1 egg yolk (it must be at room temperature), ½ teaspoon crushed sea salt flakes, ¼ teaspoon ground pepper, 1 chopped clover garlic (optional), about 1 tablespoon grainy mustard, and 2 tablespoons fresh lemon juice in a medium, high-sided bowl. Have ready an electric beater or balloon whisk. Mix together ½ cup moderately flavorful extra-virgin olive oil with ½ cup grapeseed or peanut oil. Add this oil, in a gradual drizzle, using one hand, while whisking constantly with the other. The yolk-oil mixture will stiffen and then relax into a rich emulsion sauce that will keep its shape and gloss. Use, ideally within the day, as a sauce, dip, spread, or accompaniment to soft-cooked eggs, salad leaves, sliced tomatoes, or warm potatoes. With freshly cooked crab or lobster, this mayonnaise is celestial.

Note: Pregnant women, immune-damaged individuals, as well as the very young or elderly, should avoid eating real mayonnaise.

Marinating olives

Salt-cured olives can be mellowed, aromatized, plumped up, and preserved using heated extra-virgin olive oil as a marinade. Pack 1¼ to 1½ cups dried black olives into a heatproof, 2-cup glass container. Set the container on a heatproof surface. Push in some sturdy fresh herbs, such as rosemary, bay, and oregano, and add some spices, citrus zest, and peppercorns. Heat 1 cup extra-virgin olive oil to 375°F and pour it over the olives, just to overflowing, keeping your hands clear: It will splutter. The oil will actually "cook" the olives. Let cool, cover, and seal. Use the aromatized olives after 2 days, and they will keep for up to 2 months.

spaghetti with olive oil and garlic

One of the simplest, most perfect dishes ever: pasta dressed with garlicky, chile-spiked olive oil. You can finish the dish off with fresh herbs and Parmesan, if you like, but all that really matters is the effect of the oil on the pasta. Use a first, cold-pressed extra-virgin olive oil, if you can.

Serves 4

Ingredients

9 ounces dried spaghetti
Salt
2 cloves garlic, slivered
5 tablespoons extra-virgin olive oil
½ to 1 teaspoon dried red chile
  flakes
Sea salt flakes and freshly ground
  black pepper

Method

1. Cook the pasta in lots of boiling, salted water, according to the package instructions or until *al dente*. Drain, reserving 2 tablespoons of the cooking water.
2. Heat 3 tablespoons of the oil in the still-hot, empty pot. Add the garlic and cook gently, but do not allow it to color.
3. Stir in the chile flakes, then the hot pasta and the reserved cooking liquid. Toss all together, adding sea salt and black pepper to taste.
4. Serve the pasta hot, with the remaining oil drizzled over the top.

fats

Fats act as enrichers, they preserve, they help create flaky layers in pastries, they thicken watery liquids. They also taste good in their own right: Butter, melted, is one of the simplest sauces ever. Fat from drippings, lard, and goose fat were once lambasted because they are saturated fats, but they are being reevaluated as some of the most honorable, delicious, and perhaps even heart-healthy foods. Even so, being rich, calorific, and slow to digest, fats should be used in moderation.

Fats carry distinctive flavors of their own, but may also absorb those of adjacent foods: Store them in a cool, dark place, ideally in opaque containers or wrappers. Sunlight damages fats, creating off-flavors over time.

1 Ghee This dense, clarified butter fat is made by heating cows' milk until some of the milk solids caramelize and the water evaporates off. It tastes uniquely toasty, it does not burn, and it has a long shelf life. Ghee distinguishes many Asian dishes, including breads, desserts, and grain dishes, and is used in tempering Indian spices.

2 Goose fat This soft, creamy, and fragrant fat is produced naturally by the rendering of goose carcasses. The best versions are usually from rural France. Use the fat in confits, pâtés, and cassoulets, or for frying or roasting potatoes.

3 Shredded suet Machine-shredded beef (or mutton) kidney fat, suet adds flavor to doughs, batters, dumplings, cakes, and puddings.

Traditional in sweet British mince-meat, suet also excels in steamed suet puddings.

4 Drippings This naturally tasty rendered fat from beef is creamy and full of flavor when made well. Use it when cooking beef casseroles, to grate into dumplings for stews, or to sauté potatoes.

5 Lard This white pork fat is superb combined with butter in shortcrust pastry, but is most useful as a frying medium. With a high smoke point, lard is great for sautéing pork or bacon for stews, or for deep-frying fritters. Good-quality lard can also be used to add flavor to pea or cabbage soups.

6 Butter Whether it's used for spreading or cooking, butter is only

as good as the cream from which it is made. There are two main types. Sweetcream butter (a), the most popular in Britain and the United States, is made by churning pasteurized cream, and may be salted or unsalted. Lactic butter (b), usually unsalted, is popular in continental Europe; it is made by adding a lactic culture to the cream before it is churned. With its mild acidity, lactic butter often has more flavor than sweetcream versions. Lactic butter is great served in slivers with blue cheeses, or melted over asparagus or green beans. French butters are usually excellent, and include AOC butters (c), of guaranteed quality. Eat these in slivers with charcuterie or steak.

Store butter away from aromatic substances: It easily absorbs other flavors.

steaks with truffle butter
Serves 4

For 4 griddled beef steaks, mix together $3\frac{1}{2}$ tablespoons diced salted butter; $\frac{3}{4}$ jounce finely sliced
preserved black truffle; 4 crushed cloves garlic; 2 tablespoons chopped fresh tarragon, parsley, or chives; and
1 tablespoon fresh lemon juice. Using a fork, beat to a
paste. Spread on oiled aluminum foil and roll up into
a 4-inch cylinder. Twist the ends tightly closed. Chill for
4 hours or freeze for 30 minutes. Unwrap, cut into
slices, and set 2 slices on each hot steak.

cupcakes with lavender butter cream icing
Makes enough for 12 small cakes

Grind 1 tablespoon fresh lavender buds, 1 teaspoon
Campari bitters (or 3 drops red food coloring), and
6 sugar cubes, using a pestle and mortar or an
electric spice grinder, to a powder. Whisk this into
$3\frac{1}{2}$ tablespoons cubed, softened, unsalted butter.
Using an electric beater, gradually incorporate
$\frac{1}{2}$ cup sifted confectioners' sugar and 2 tablespoons
hot water, heated simple syrup, or hot lemon juice.
Use to decorate 12 small cakes, adding extra
lavender buds or blooms as decoration, if desired.

beurre blanc with poached salmon
Serves 4

Whisk 5 tablespoons plus 1 teaspoon cubed good-
quality unsalted butter in a bowl set over another bowl
of warm water until creamy. In a saucepan, cook
1 chopped shallot, 4 tablespoons tarragon vinegar and
4 tablespoons Sauvignon Blanc together until reduced
by half. Whisk the shallot mixture, along with 1 tablespoon heavy cream, into the soft butter, until the
consistency is mousselike. Season with salt and pepper.
Spoon this warm, creamy sauce over hot fish and serve
without delay. (Most versions whip the butter into the
reduction: This is the reverse.)

brandy butter with citrus segments in brandy snaps
Serves 4

Assemble $3\frac{1}{2}$ tablespoons softened butter; scant $\frac{1}{2}$
cup confectioners' sugar; 4 tablespoons cognac; juice
and grated zest of 1 orange; 4 brandy snap baskets;
4 clementines in Cointreau syrup. Whisk together the
butter, sugar, cognac, and some of the orange juice until
light and pale. Add the remaining juice and the zest to
taste. Spoon some into each basket and add the
clementine segments. Dust with confectioners' sugar
and orange zest, if desired. Serve within 2 hours.

milk products

While no cook doubts the deliciousness of cultured milk products, such as Greek yogurt, nor should he or she rule out the benefits of canned or long-life milks, which can be used to make respectable dishes, from caramel custard to fish chowder. Coconut milk products are also perfect pantry foods: They have a long shelf life, and add instant richness to Asian foods.

Only milk products with a high butterfat content should be heated or boiled; these include clotted cream (55 percent butterfat) and crème fraîche (35 percent). Yogurt (with a butterfat content of 8 to 10 percent) curdles if boiled, so it should be stirred into hot foods just before serving. Coconut milk products should also be cooked gently, and never boiled.

1 Coconut cream Made from pressed grated coconut, and highly calorific, coconut cream can be used in Southeast Asian and Pacific cooking, especially curries, but also works well in Indian and African dishes, such as spicy stews, rice dishes, and coconutty desserts.

2 UHT milk Long-life, or UHT (ultra-heat-treated) milk makes remarkably acceptable cheese sauce and chocolate pudding, and works well in cakes and other baked goods, too.

3 Coconut milk This is a thinner version of coconut cream and can be used in the same way.

4 Clotted cream This high-fat and dense, long-cooked cream is at its best when farm-produced in Devon or Cornwall, but it is mostly factory-made. Use it dusted with sugar and grilled for a quick crème brûlée; eat it layered with berry fruits in

alcohol; or use it, with strawberry jam, to fill a sponge cake.

5 Crème fraîche This French "fresh cream" is, in fact, a cultured product similar to sour cream. It needs no whipping and, being high in fat, is unlikely to curdle in cooked dishes (unless a low-fat version is used). It is delicious mixed with fresh fruit.

6 Greek yogurt There is no substitute for this thick, full-cream yogurt, which is curdled with bacteria and sometimes strained. Use it in dips and dressings, and in desserts—mixed with honey and pistachios, for example.

7 Creamed coconut Sold in a solid block, this is cheaper than coconut cream and keeps for longer once opened. You can make it into a coconut cream by melting it in milk or water, or else shave it directly into a dish towards the end of cooking. Use it in curries and kulfi.

8 Sweetened condensed milk This is milk that has been reduced by boiling to about one-third of its original volume. It consists of about 40 percent sugar, and is great for making fudge. When simmered (unopened, in the can) for 2 to 3 hours, it forms a dense caramel, which is superb in many Latin American, Asian, and African desserts, tarts, and ice creams.

9 Evaporated milk Reduced by evaporation to about half its original volume, evaporated milk is unsweetened. It is useful in sauces where reduction is needed, and in custards and rice puddings. Diluted with an equal quantity of water, it can replace fresh milk in cooking.

10 Dried full-fat milk Modern methods of drying mean that dried milk powders have a similar nutrient content to fresh. They are useful as a standby, for baking or sauces, and in Indian sweetmeats.

cheeses

Cheese has great significance in Europe and the Americas, less so in other parts of the world. At its best, cheese is a "live" food that, thanks to helpful enzymes and microorganisms, is in a state of continuous development. Thousands of cheeses exist, from very young, soft, and mild cheeses to old, hard, and pungent ones. The fat content varies from 1 to 75 percent, but the protein levels are consistently high, making cheese an invaluable food and ingredient.

For the best cheese, find a retailer (or *affineur*) who keeps his or her cheeses in a cold, moist environment, allowing them to continue aging naturally. Most cheese sold in the shops is stored in refrigerated cabinets, which are too cold for the aging process to continue.

1 Feta This creamy but crumbly, brine-ripened cheese from Greece is best made from mixed sheep's and goats' milk, but is now usually made of cows' milk. Buy only Greek versions, which may be young (very soft), medium (firmer), or old (saltier, denser), and are best when *apo varelli* (meaning "from the tub"). Dot it over salads, or mash it to a paste with oil, garlic, and mint.

2 Manchego Spain's most famous hard cheese, Manchego is made from sheep's milk and pressed into patterned molds. It is sold either as fresh (*fresco*), slightly aged (*curado*), or older than three months (*viejo*). A full-fat cheese, with a creamy, firm interior, it is superb eaten with membrillo. Or try it sliced over roasted peppers or grated over vegetable soup.

3 Roquefort This noble French blue cheese, made from sheep's milk, is creamy, pungent, and intense, but sweet, and with a silky mouth feel. It is superb both as a dessert, served with fresh berries, for example, and in cooking: Mash it to a paste with cognac and butter; slice and melt it over beef steaks; or add cream and melt it over piping-hot pasta.

4 Farmhouse Cheddar The world's most copied cows' milk cheese is epicurean when cloth-wrapped and farm-made, and usually acceptable when factory-made. A dense but flaky cheese, Cheddar is superb in many situations, but particularly grated into sauces—for cauliflower, for example—and in soufflés.

5 Fromage frais This mild and soft, unripened cheese, with a fat content of 0 to 8 percent, can be used like yogurt, in cold desserts such as fools and ice creams, as well as in dressings: Mixed with a little seasoning, vinegar, and olive oil, it goes beautifully with watercress or chicory.

If adding fromage frais to a hot sauce, make sure you do it right at the end, to avoid curdling.

6 Crottin de Chavignol These small, fresh goats' milk cheeses from France are waxy with chalky centers and natural rinds, and shrink and become more pungent as they age. The cheese melts seductively when it is halved or sliced onto toast and grilled, or when shaved over hot rice, pasta, or gnocchi.

7 Parmesan In English, the term *Parmesan cheese* is sometimes used to describe any Italian hard cheese used for grating, but in Italy the generic name for these cheeses is *grana*; Parmesan—which is the abbreviated anglicization of grana Parmigiano-Reggiano—is the best known version; grana padano is another. Made of unpasteurized cows' milk and matured for up to four years, grana has an intense fragrance and a flaky, grainy texture.

Buy small, rough-cut chunks that you can grate as needed, over risotto and pasta, or sliver and eat with Parma ham or other cured meats as part of an antipasto. Parmesan also goes beautifully with ripe figs, peaches, and pears.

8 Mozzarella This famously stretchy Italian whey cheese is made from cows' or, preferably, buffalos' milk. The curds are kneaded in whey until stretchy, and then hand-shaped into balls or braids; these should always be sold packed in liquid. When really fresh, mozzarella tastes pleasantly milky and mild. (Beware porous, compressed blocks of so-called pizza mozzarella, usually

made outside Italy.) Traditionally sliced in a salad with tomatoes, basil, and olive oil, or melted on pizza or in calzones, mozzarella also tastes great layered with avocado and anchovies on garlicky bruschetta.

9 Emmental This unpasteurized cows' milk cheese, with its distinctive holes, is Swiss in origin but now made elsewhere in Europe, often in France. It is creamy, with a rubbery texture and sweet, fruity taste. Emmental is great to cook with. Better cubed than grated, it forms stretchy strands when heated, and is excellent in gratins, soufflés, and fondues. Thinly sliced, it melts wonderfully over potatoes and gnocchi.

storage

Try to buy characterful cheeses little and often. Wrap them, loosely, in waxed paper rather than plastic, which causes cheese to sweat. Store cheeses in the fridge or a cool, dark, and well-ventilated place, isolated from other foods, since they both absorb and transmit flavors.

parmesan "tuiles" with cheese cream

Makes 20; serves 6

Preheat the oven to 425°F. On an oiled baking sheet, place 4 piles of 1 tablespoon each coarsely grated Parmesan cheese. Bake for 3½ to 5 minutes until melted and golden. Use a palette knife to slide each hot tuile off the baking sheet. Quickly lay them over the side of a small clean jar to cool. Repeat until you have 20 tuiles. Beat 3½ ounces Roquefort or Gorgonzola cheese together with ¼ cup cream cheese, 2 tablespoons fino sherry, and 2 tablespoons chopped fresh chives. Fill the tuiles with the cheese mixture. Serve with chilled fino sherry.

twice-baked goat cheese soufflés

Stephanie Alexander—a legendary Australian cook and author—gives us this marvelous recipe, which uses goat cheese in a very new way. The soufflés are not served in their dishes, so you can use any kind of mold, even teacups, as long as they hold about two-thirds of a cup.

Serves 6

Ingredients

5½ tablespoons butter
6 tablespoons flour
1½ cups warm milk
2½ ounces fresh goat cheese
1 tablespoon freshly grated
   Parmesan cheese
2 tablespoons choppped fresh
   parsley
3 egg yolks
Salt and freshly ground black
   pepper
4 egg whites
2 cups heavy cream

Method

1. Preheat the oven to 350°F. Melt 1½ tablespoons of the butter and use it to grease 6 ⅔-cup individual heatproof soufflé molds. Melt the remaining butter in a small, heavy-bottom saucepan. Stir in the flour and cook over a medium heat, stirring for 2 minutes.
2. Gradually add the milk, stirring constantly. Bring to a boil, then reduce the heat and simmer for 5 minutes.
3. Mash the goat cheese until soft and add it to the hot milk mixture, along with the Parmesan cheese and parsley. Remove from the heat and let cool for a few minutes. Fold in the egg yolks thoroughly and season with salt and pepper.
4. In a separate bowl, beat the egg whites until frothy, then fold them quickly and lightly into the cheese mixture. Divide the mixture among the prepared molds and smooth the surface of each.
5. Stand the molds in a baking dish lined with a tea towel and pour in boiling water to come two-thirds up the sides of the molds. Bake for about 20 minutes, until firm to the touch and well puffed.
6. Allow the soufflés to rest for a minute or so (they will deflate when they come out of the oven), then gently ease them out of the molds. Invert them on to a plate covered with plastic wrap and set aside until needed.
7. To serve, preheat the oven to 350°F. Place the soufflés in a buttered baking dish so that they are not touching. Pour the cream over (about one-third cup per soufflé). Place in the oven for 15 minutes. The soufflés will look swollen and golden. Serve with the cream from the baking dish or with fresh tomato sauce.

grains, legumes, & nuts

grains and meals

Grains, usually the seeds of grasslike plants, as well as their many derivatives, are among the world's most essential staple foods. Imagine life without pancakes or porridge, baguettes, or blinis. Whether we use them whole, cracked, rolled, or popped, grain foods can create an inexhaustible range of superb dishes. Furthermore, they are perfect ingredients: They have a long shelf life, they transport easily, they are affordable and adaptable, and they are hugely nutritious. Included here, too, are meals, such as trahana and gari, which are not grains but are similar in their uses.

Dried grains are meant to keep, but they deteriorate over time. Use them within six months, before their natural oil turns rancid, a year at the most. Never mix a new batch with an old batch.

1 Barley couscous Less common than wheat couscous (see no. 5), these finely rolled grain fragments are treated in a similar way. Steam or sauté them and use them as a warm salad with garlic, aromatics, and herbs.

2 Pearl barley While pot barley is barley which has some of its bran removed, pearl barley has almost no bran at all: so it cooks faster (in 1 to 1½ hours). Use it for vegetable soups, or Scottish cock-a-leekie soup, to which it adds a soothing gelatinous texture. Or cook it until tender in several times its volume of water, drain, and serve dressed with yogurt, mint, and seasonings.

3 Pinhead oats When processed, oats produce oatmeal in various grades, from superfine (which cooks quickly and is a good thickener) to pinhead. The biggest

and coarsest, pinhead oats cook slowly but make delicious porridge, and are good in stuffing.

4 Rolled oats Also known as porridge oats or oatflakes, rolled oats are made from dehusked oats (or groats), which are then steam-softened and rolled. Large jumbo oats (a) are often used in muesli. Smaller porridge oats (b), rolled pinhead oats, are quicker for making porridge than normal pinhead oats (taking just five minutes

to cook), but have less flavor; they are tastier if dry-toasted first.

Use rolled oat for flapjacks, or to coat filleted herrings or mackerel before frying in bacon fat.

5 Couscous Traditionally, this North African staple consists of coarsely ground hard semolina wheat, but most of what is available is a kind of granular semolina pasta, which has been precooked, and needs only to be steamed or left to stand in boiling water. Drizzled with butter or olive oil, and flavored with spices, herbs, and perhaps harissa, couscous is superb served with lamb, fish, or vegetable tagines.

6 Semolina Coarsely milled durum wheat, semolina, or finer semolina flour, are used to make pasta and gnocchi, though they are too hard to work into a dough at home unless combined with softer flours (see pages 136–137). But semolina can also be used (with sugar, vanilla, and milk) to make sweet puddings or complex Indian sweets.

7 Ebly® wheat A partially processed, relatively new "designed" product, Ebly® wheat is durum wheat made tender enough to be cooked like rice. Interesting, chewy and adaptable, it can be cooked straight, in boiling water, or as for risotto (see page 108). Add butter, olive oil, or cream, and then serve it with chicken, fish, tofu, or precooked ham or bacon.

8 Trahana This large-crumbed grain product is popular in Greece and Turkey, but is used in some form in other countries, too. It is made from crushed wheat or flour, which is mixed with yogurt and then left to sour before being air- or sun-dried. Trahana should be rehydrated in boiling stock, water, or milk. Use it in soups, pilaffs, and stews, seasoned appropriately using soy sauce, garlic or fresh herbs, and dampened with olive oil or butter. Or, add honey and nuts and serve it as a dessert.

9 Bulghur wheat Adaptable, easy to use, and tasty, this nutty cereal product (known also as burghul or cracked wheat) is used widely in Europe and the Middle East. Consisting of wheat grain that has been parboiled, dried, and then "cracked," it can be either boiled briefly in seasoned liquid or simply left to stand while the boiling liquid is absorbed. The grains readily absorb lemon juice and olive oil, too. The basis of tabbouleh, bulghur wheat is also useful in stuffings and kibbeh.

10 Hominy grits These dried and hulled maize kernels, high in fiber, are popular in the southern United States. They are most commonly eaten ground, as grits, as a savory breakfast "mash" with bacon and eggs. They can also be used, like other ground cereals, in breads and puddings.

11 Cornmeal This maize meal, naturally golden (pictured), blue, or white, is an important staple in the Mediterranean, parts of the United States, and the Caribbean. American cornmeal is finely ground and is perfect for making muffins and cakes. Polenta, the northern Italian staple, is coarsely ground cornmeal; it becomes creamy when boiled in water, but sets hard when cooled, and can be broiled, baked, or fried.

Fine and coarse cornmeals can both be used in breads, cakes, and batters, but the texture of the baked goods will vary according to the coarseness of the meal.

12 Buckwheat Nutty, angular buckwheat seeds are not a grain, in fact (they are related to rhubarb), but are regarded as a "pseudo-cereal".

Associated traditionally with eastern Europe, buckwheat is used to make *kasha*, a Russian porridge-like dish that is served, usually, with wild mushrooms and sour cream. Cooked in sweet stock, with cherries, kirsch, and whipped cream stirred in, buckwheat makes a delicious dessert.

Buckwheat is also ground into flour (see page 136).

13 Gari Dried cassava meal rather than a grain, gari is granular and starchy, so is not dissimilar to a cereal. It is much loved in Brazil (where it is known as *farinha de mandioca*) and the West Indies. Boiled, gari makes a kind of meal porridge, which can be served with stews. In Brazil, *farinha de mandioca* is sautéed in bacon fat, butter, or palm oil, and then sprinkled over cooked foods before serving.

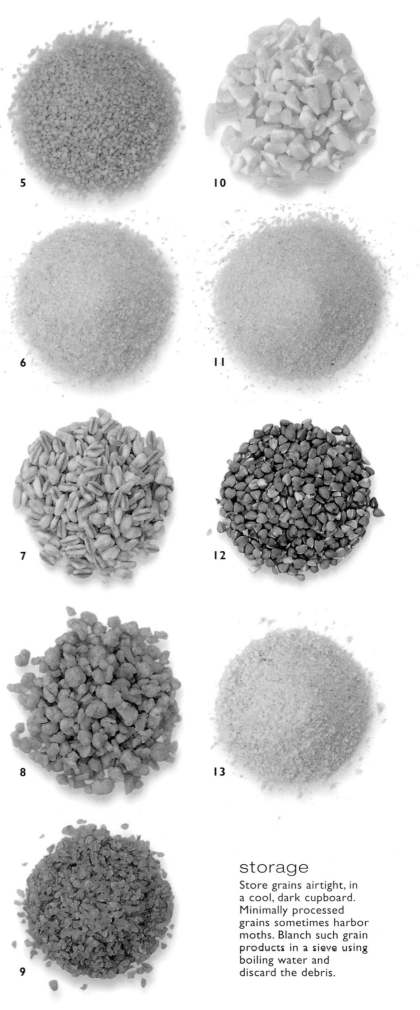

storage

Store grains airtight, in a cool, dark cupboard. Minimally processed grains sometimes harbor moths. Blanch such grain products in a sieve using boiling water and discard the debris.

cooking rice

Everyone has their favorite way to cook rice. The basic method for cooking any kind of rice is in a large amount of boiling salted water, but each type of rice has its own traditional method. Some cooks advocate rinsing rice, to remove any surface starch (which can cause the grains to clump), but this is not necessary with most mass-produced rice. Soaking rice can reduce the cooking time, and help the grains to keep their shape, but for most types of rice this is strictly optional.

1

2

1

2

3

4

3

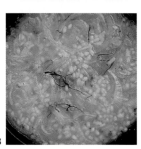
4

Cooking basmati rice
The simplest way to cook basmati rice is by the 2:1 absorption method. Put the rice, in cupfuls, in the pan (with spices, if you like) and pour in twice as many cupfuls of boiling water. Bring to a boil, cover, turn down the heat as low as possible, and cook for 10 to 12 minutes, without stirring, until all the water has been absorbed, and the rice is tender.

Cooking paella rice
Although paella rice is short-grained, like risotto rice, it is cooked differently. After coating the rice in hot fat in the pan, you simply pour in boiling water (or stock) to cover generously. Keep extra boiling water on hand, which you can add if the rice looks dry. Use a spatula to check that the rice isn't sticking, but don't stir it. Add saffron toward the end, before adding other ingredients.

Cooking risotto rice
Once you have fried the onions and any other aromatics in oil or butter, add the rice and fry it for a minute or so in the oil, which will help keep the grains separate. Add wine, for extra flavor, and when that has evaporated off, add hot stock by the ladleful, waiting for the liquid to absorb before adding the next one, until the rice is tender. This will take 20 to 30 minutes.

Making rice pudding
The stubby grains of pudding rice are transformed into a creamy, sticky mellowness when cooked slowly in vanilla-infused, sweetened milk. Follow the simple recipe on page 111. It may seem impossible that such a small amount of rice can thicken so much milk, but it does. And any milk that is still liquid solidifies when the pudding is cold.

handkerchief sushi

You can make these pretty, unconventional sushi shapes by using a twist of clean muslin or plastic wrap, and your preferred flavorings and decorations. Heresy it may seem, but, if no Japanese sushi rice can be found, pudding rice is a passable imitation; it will just need extra liquid.

Serves 4 as a starter

Ingredients
1 teaspoon dashi stock granules
6 ounces Japanese sushi rice, soaked, rinsed, and drained
1 teaspoon pureed garlic
1 teaspoon pureed ginger
2 tablespoons mirin
4 teaspoons rice vinegar

Fillings
6 umeboshi plums, quartered (or 4 tablespoons umeboshi paste), or
1¾ ounces canned clams, crab, smoked mackerel, or salmon, drained, or 3 tablespoons miso or bean paste

Garnishes
Nori seaweed; cured salmon or trout roe; strips of chives or scallions; strips or slices of red or green chiles; and/or tiny sprigs parsley or chervil

Method
1. In a large pan, dissolve the stock granules in scant 1 cup boiling water (or make the stock by traditional methods).
2. Add the rice to the stock in a pan, and bring to a boil.
3. Reduce the heat to maintain a simmer, cover and cook undisturbed for 10 to 12 minutes, until the liquid is absorbed and the rice is tender and sticky.
4. Add the next 4 ingredients, stir, then tip the seasoned rice out onto a tray. Fan it until cool enough to handle.
5. Divide the rice into 16 to 24 balls. Using clean hands, pick up one rice ball, push some filling deep inside, then close it.
6. Create a garnish on the opposite side of the ball. Roll the ball up in plastic wrap, twisting it tightly underneath. Continue until all are made, then unwrap.
7. Serve the sushi with pickled ginger, mixed or ready-made wasabi, and tamari (Japanese soy sauce). Eat using chopsticks or your fingers.

rice

The staple food of roughly half the world's peoples, and essential in key dishes from Spanish paella to Japanese sushi, rice is absolutely universal. The success of any rice dish depends on choosing the right rice and the appropriate cooking method. There are thousands of varieties of rice, a cereal grass, but most can be graded into long- or short-grained types: The former, such as basmati, is the best rice for eating plain, while more absorbent short-grain rice is suited to dishes like risotto. Most cultures eat white (that is, dehusked) rice, even though brown or whole grain rice (with the husk left on) is more nutritious.

Buy good-quality rice, which cooks well and has grains that stay separate. Look for clean, unbroken, and similar-sized grains and clear classification: Arborio or Vialone Nano rice is much better than anything labeled simply 'risotto rice.'

Store rice airtight, in a dark cupboard, and use within six months.

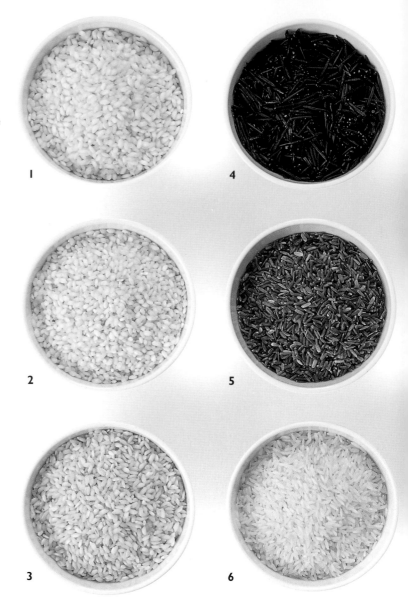

1 Arborio rice This is the best-known Italian risotto rice and graded as Superfine. Its fat, oval grains absorb much liquid without softening excessively, swell plumply, and taste nutty. Cook as risotto with butter and/or oil, onions, aromatics, and hot stock. Cold risotto can be used to make fish cakes or suppli (crumbed, deep-fried rice balls), or to stuff tomatoes.

2 Vialone Nano rice Classified as Semifine, Vialone Nano is a hybrid and has smaller grains and a nuttier bite than Arborio. It also takes longer to cook, is creamier and more expensive. The gourmet's choice for risotto, Vialone Nano cooks superbly with rich stock, game, wild mushrooms, and garlic.

3 Carnaroli rice A Superfine rice, like Arborio, but less common and far superior, Carnaroli keeps a firm *al dente* bite in risotto. Cook it with saffron, white wine, and shavings of Parmesan, for example, or with added prawns, scallops, or squid for seafood risotto.

4 Wild rice Not a rice, or even a grain, wild rice is a grass grown mainly in Canada and the north-western United States. The long, dark grains have a gorgeously nutty and chewy texture. If soaked overnight, the rice takes about 25 minutes to cook; up to twice that if unsoaked. Cook it until the grains split to reveal their brown interior but are still chewy. Serve with butter, fruit vinegars, or nut oils, or use in stuffings and fritters.

5 Carmargue red rice Originally from the marshy areas of the Camargue, in southern France, this reddish grain is a prized ingredient. It tastes rather like buckwheat. Durable, it takes up to 45 minutes to cook, although presoaking can shorten this time. Add bacon or duck fat, and serve it with intense herbed garlicky dressings; it goes well with rich meats and game.

7

8

9

Arkansas, the Carolinas, and Mississippi.) American long-grain works well as an side dish or in seafood pilaffs.

7 Calasparra rice This classic, top-quality Spanish paella rice is very absorbent and cooks clean, until the stubby and hard grains are plump and tender, but not creamy. Use for paella (which should be cooked, uncovered, in a wide shallow pan: see page 108) or as stuffing for tomatoes and bell peppers.

8 Quick-cook whole grain rice While most whole grain, or brown, rice takes a long time to cook, quick-cook versions take just 10 to12 minutes, and are remarkably tasty. Serve it plain as an accompaniment, or add garlic, olive or nut oil, or just butter and cheese. It also works well in stuffings and risotto.

9 Pudding rice This stubby, inexpensive rice swells during cooking, and is perfect for milky rice pudding (see page 108). Although unorthodox, pudding rice can also be used for sushi (cooled, seasoned, and shaped into snacks) or even risotto.

10 Basmati rice This famous, long-grain Asian rice is prized by cooks in India, Pakistan, and Bangladesh and is enjoyed around the world as the classic accompaniment. It cooks quickly and gives an elegantly separate, scented, and delicious result. Basmati is superb cooked with cinnamon, cardamom, and bay, and can be used in buttery, sweet Persian chellous (pilaff), Indian birianis, or even salads.

11 Thai jasmine rice Also known as fragrant rice, this slim-grained but faintly sticky Asian rice is beloved of Thais and Vietnamese. It has a delicate scent when cooked, and clumps pleasantly. Cook it simply, by the absorption method (see page 108) or traditionally, and use with green and red coconutty Thai curries, fish and vegetable stews, or stir-fries.

12 Black glutinous rice This sticky Asian rice is used in Thai and Balinese desserts, as well as in savory dishes, and is often served densely compressed, wrapped in leaves. Cook it in coconut milk, with berries and coconut cream, or in dumplings and wraps.

13 Sushi rice This famous slightly sticky, short-grained Japanese rice has a clean aroma when cooked and a pearly, nutty appeal. Seasoned and sweetened, it is often compressed into sushi, enclosed in nori sheets or other wrappers. The rice should be cooked using only little water.

14 Bhutan red and green rice These naturally colored, chewy rices from Bhutan (also known as Imperial red or Imperial green rice) evolved during the Ming period (fourteenth to seventeenth centuries), when they were prized for their nutritional value. Flavorful but rather slow to cook (taking 30 to 50 minutes), this rice absorbs three or more times its volume of liquid.

Serve Bhutan red rice (a) with rich red meats, poultry stews, vegetable curries, or as a salad. Bhutan green rice (b) goes well with lots of garlic and fresh herbs, unfiltered extra-virgin olive oil, and avocado. Or toss it with minimally cooked greens using virgin nut oils and lime.

6 American long-grain rice Also known as Carolina rice, American long-grain rice is one of the most popular all-purpose rices. The grains cook clean, tasty, and separate, in around 12 minutes, and have an almost popcornlike taste if they are of good quality. (Some of the best long-grain rice comes from

12

13

14a

14b

lionhead rice-pork balls
Serves 4

Microwave 8 ounces black glutinous rice with 1½ cups boiling water, covered, on high power for 20 minutes. Drain, reserving scant ½ cup of the water. Mix one-third of the rice with 9 ounces food-processed bacon and chicken mixture, adding 1 tablespoon rice flour, 2 teaspoons pureed garlic, 4 tablespoons grated onion and 4 tablespoons chopped broccoli, and 2 tablespoons chicken broth, Process again. Shape into 24 balls. Wet and coat each in some of the rice. Microwave, covered, for 20 minutes, until tender but firm. Boil the reserved cooking water with some rice vinegar, five-spice powder, sugar, and soy sauce to make a dipping sauce, and serve with the remaining rice.

spanish rice with seafood
Serves 4

Sauté 12 ounces Spanish paella rice in a wide shallow pan with 4 tablespoons olive oil, 4 sliced cloves garlic, 2 onions, and some sea salt. After 3 minutes, stir in 4¼ cups fish stock. Cook over medium heat for 15 to 18 minutes, then add 12 raw prawn tails, 24 small clams, a handful chopped green beans, and ⅛ teaspoon powdered saffron. Cook for 4 minutes more, until the rice is tender, turning the seafood at intervals. Add lemon juice and serve hot.

risotto with pesto
Serves 4

In a large shallow pan, heat 5 tablespoons butter with 1 chopped onion and 2 chopped cloves garlic. Stir in 9 ounces risotto rice. Add 7 tablespoons dry white vermouth: let it bubble off and evaporate. Ladle in 1 cup hot chicken stock. Cook over medium heat for 18 minutes, adding more hot stock at roughly 6-minute intervals. Season using ⅓ cup fresh pesto. Cook for 5 to 8 minutes longer, until soupy and the rice is tender. Serve with freshly grated Parmesan cheese, some fresh basil, and freshly ground black pepper.

vanilla rice pudding
Serves 4

Boil 2½ cups light cream with 1½ cups milk and pour over 2 sugar cubes with vanilla seeds (see page 16), the split vanilla pod itself, 2½ ounces pudding rice, and ⅓ cup sugar in a large heatproof baking dish. Stir well. Bake at 325°F, uncovered, for 3 to 4 hours. Alternatively, cook in a microwave oven on high power for 15 minutes (covered), stir, reduce the power to medium, and cook (covered) for a further 25 minutes. The liquid should be creamy and the rice soft. Sprinkle 5 teaspoons muscovado sugar on top and broil until golden and crusty. Serve hot, with cream.

bacon, barley, and wheat chowder

Barley and wheat grains give this substantial soup-stew its pleasant texture and body. Although Ebly® wheat is normally a rapidly cooked, "instant" grain, in this recipe it is cooked slowly to add richness. With the bacon and other vegetables, this dish becomes a well-balanced meal-in-a-plate.

Serves 4–6

Ingredients
1 pound, 10 ounces rolled, smoked bacon, in one piece
1 bay leaf
1 handful fresh thyme
2 onions, halved
1¾ ounces each pot barley, pearl barley, and Ebly® wheat grains
8 small potatoes, peeled
6 ribs celery, very coarsely chopped
1 sweet potato, peeled
1 ham stock bouillon cube, crumbled
Light cream or milk
3½ tablespoons butter
5 tablespoons flour
12 ounces canned sweet corn, drained
Salt and freshly ground black pepper

Method
1. In a large saucepan, put the bacon with the bay leaf, thyme, and onions and 1½ quarts water. Bring to a boil, reduce the heat, and simmer for 45 minutes, partly covered.
2. Add the barleys and wheat grains, the potatoes, celery, and sweet potato. Simmer for 45 minutes.
3. Pour off the liquid, reserving 2½ to 3 cups of it. Add the bouillon cube to the reserved liquid, and add enough cream to make 4¼ cups.
4. In a second saucepan, melt the butter. Stir in the flour, then whisk in the liquid, stirring, to make a creamy sauce.
5. Remove the sweet potato and the bacon from the grains mixture and cut them into bite-size chunks. Return them to the pan, along with the corn.
6. Add the creamy sauce to the pan. Season to taste with salt (if necessary) and black pepper. Reheat and serve the chowder hot in large bowls, with fresh herbs and seasonings as desired.

legumes

The seeds of leguminous plants—peas, beans, and lentils—are delicious and have been a staple for millennia. Used whole, split, husked, cracked, or ground, legumes dry and store well and are high in protein. Dried beans, which must usually be soaked before cooking, have the best taste and texture, but good-quality precooked, canned beans are useful when time is short. Dried beans must be boiled hard for ten minutes at the start of cooking, to inactivate potentially lethal toxins.

1 Beans The dried beans of the *Phaseolus vulgaris* species, native to Central America, are the most common legumes used in the West. The many varieties of beans vary subtly in taste and texture but they can be treated in similar ways, and are all available dry or canned. If dry, they require soaking then cooking for 30 to 60 minutes.

Glossy **red kidney beans** (a), famously used in chili con carne and feijoada, go well with chiles and garlic. They can be blended in stock to make soup, mixed with rice, or added whole to casseroles.

Black beans (b) are popular in Brazil and Mexico, especially in stews, and have a strong and meaty taste. Italians prefer pink, speckly **borlotti beans** (c) and white **cannellini beans** (d) for soups and stews.

Pale green **flageolet beans** (e) are prized in France. They go well

with lamb, whose juices they absorb beautifully. Small white beans known as **navy beans** (f) hold their shape well and cook to a lovely creamy consistency; use them in soups and stews, with roasts, or in ham casseroles. The same beans are doused in tomato sauce and sold as **baked beans** (g), which are eaten on toast in millions of British households. **Pinto beans** (h), loved in Mexico and Spain, are good for mashed "refried" beans, and can be bought canned in chile sauce.

2 Fava beans These large, white, kidney-shaped beans are popular all around the Mediterranean. After soaking, they should be cooked for about 1 hour. They are excellent with sausage, including chorizo, herbs, and fresh tomatoes. Giant fava beans, called *gigantes*, are prized in Greece, and are now available in cans. Serve them either

heated up or cold with lamb or chicken, or as a salad.

3 Ful medames North African beans, very popular in Egypt, ful medames usually need cooking for up to 2 hours if bought dry. Add spices, olive oil, and herbs (such as mint or parsley) to the beans toward the end of cooking, and serve them with flatbreads. Mashed to a paste, ful medames can be pushed inside pita pockets along with crunchy pickles: a quick meal if you buy the canned type (pictured).

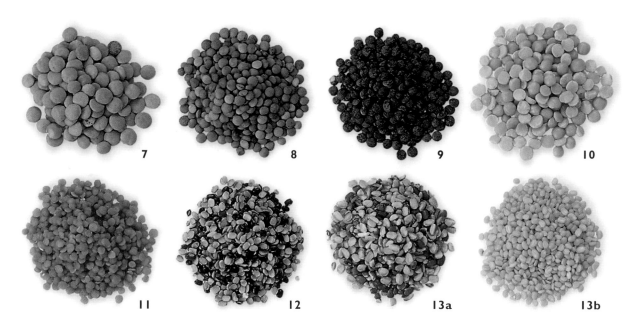

7   8   9   10

11   12   13a   13b

4 Black-eyed peas These creamy beans with black "eyes," a variety of cowpea, are greatly loved in India, Mexico, the Caribbean, and the United States, where they feature in Creole dishes. Nutty tasting, they go well with coconut, chiles, coriander and pork, and also make superb savory bean cakes.

5 Aduki beans In China and Japan, these small, mild-tasting beans are often used as a sweet filling for steamed buns or dumplings. They are good mixed with other beans and aromatics, and with rice. Add them to salads, casseroles, soups, or noodle dishes.

6 Chickpeas (garbanzo beans) These legumes are vital to Spanish, Latin American, Middle Eastern, and Indian cooking. Dried chickpeas (pictured) are best used in spicy stews, but canned chickpeas are more convenient for mashing to a creamy puree to mix with tahini, olive oil, garlic, and lemon juice for hummus. Falafel is made from dried chickpeas, soaked but not cooked, and ground together with herbs, spices, and garlic, and fried.

7 Green lentils These split lentils are the basis of millions of dal-roti (lentils and bread) meals all over Asia. You do not need to soak them, but

if you do, you can halve the cooking time to 20 minutes. Good with garlic, chiles, and bay leaves, green lentils cook to a semisoft mush, perfect for a soup or stew.

8 Umbrian lentils These brownish lentils from Umbria, in Italy, are delicious cooked (unsoaked) for 20 to 30 minutes with onion, garlic, celery, and herbs, and served with bread, rice, or pasta. Add butter or olive oil and balsamic vinegar before serving.

9 Puy lentils These highly regarded French lentils can be cooked, unsoaked, in 15 to 20 minutes, and are deliciously nutty. They suit garlic, herbs, and olive oil, and taste good with duck or goose fat, or garlicky vinaigrette, especially one based on balsamic or sherry vinegar. Serve as a salad or side dish.

10 Yellow split peas Used world-wide in dhals, stews, soups, and fritters, in Europe these peas are often turned into soups (with ham or bacon). Needing no soaking, they cook quickly to a mush. Ground dry to a powder, they act as an instant thickener.

11 Split red lentils Grown world-wide, split red lentils are known under many different names, including

masoor dal. They are loved for their color, mellow taste, 20-minute cooking time, and ability to absorb flavors. Use them in spicy stews, vegetable curries, and soups; in small amounts, they act as a thickener.

12 Black gram (urad) This valuable pulse is used with great ingenuity in India, either whole, split, or skinned. Split black gram (pictured), called *urad dal chilka* in India, is famous as the basis of many purees, which are known, confusingly, as dal, or dhal. It doesn't need soaking, but requires longer cooking than most small legumes. Small amounts of whole black gram, tempered in hot oil and spices, can be used as a seasoning to pour over rice.

13 Mung beans (green gram) Dried mung beans, popular all over Asia, are sold whole, split (a), in which case they are called *moong dal chilka*, or skinned (b), as *moong dal.* The beans should be soaked for 2 hours and then cooked for 15 to 20 minutes. Use them with salty-sweet or spicy accompaniments, in Asian-style rice dishes or in dumplings, ground up with seasonings, garlic, and yogurt.

14 Tofu (bean curd) Best-known under its Chinese name, tofu, this soybean "cheese" is soft, high in protein and low in calories, but also low in taste, so it needs assertive seasoning. Fresh tofu (a), which is best marinated before cooking, is good with garlic, ginger, soy sauce, and black bean flavors. Use it instead of egg or cheese to add a protein boost to vegetable, rice, and noodle dishes. Silken tofu (b) has a longer shelf life (it keeps, unopened, for a year or so), it is softer, and it goes well in Asian-style soups, purees, and sauces. Try it also with fruit, in blended smoothies.

14a   14b

lamb dhansak

Lentils are a staple of Indian cooking, and in this delicious recipe the talented Indian author, Monisha Bharadwaj, uses them with lamb, spices, and seeds in an authentic Parsee dish.

Serves 4

Ingredients

10 ounces lamb stew meat, trimmed and cubed
5 ounces split yellow lentils
5 ounces butternut squash, finely chopped
2 large onions, diced
1 large tomato, chopped
6 tablespoons each chopped fresh cilantro leaves and chopped fresh mint leaves
4 tablespoons diced red pumpkin
4 tablespoons chopped fresh fenugreek leaves
1 teaspoon turmeric powder
1 teaspoon chile powder
1 teaspoon sugar
Salt to taste
4 tablespoons white distilled vinegar
1 tablespoon sunflower oil
1 teaspoon cumin seeds

Method

1. Put all the ingredients listed from lamb to salt in a heavy-bottom saucepan with 2 cups water, and cook at a simmer until the lamb is tender and the lentils are soft.

2. Mash the vegetables and lentils with a wooden spoon, taking care not to break up the meat. Stir in the vinegar.

3. Heat the oil in a frying pan and fry the cumin seeds. Pour the oil and cumin over the lamb mixture.

4. Simmer for 5 minutes, then serve the curry hot, with rice or Indian breads.

lentil chermoula soup with garlic scallops

This superb soup recipe from Paul Gayler, the prestigious executive chef at London's Lanesborough Hotel, shows off Puy lentils at their best. This is a hearty soup with fragrant Moroccan spices, topped with buttered, garlicky scallops. Prawns could replace the scallops, if preferred.

Serves 4

Ingredients

For the soup
4 tablespoons olive oil
1 small onion, chopped
1 clove garlic, crushed
½-inch piece ginger, peeled and finely chopped
½ teaspoon ground cumin
½ teaspoon ground coriander
1 small red bell pepper, seeded and chopped
3 ripe plum tomatoes, chopped
1 teaspoon harissa paste
1 cup Puy lentils, rinsed and drained
1 quart chicken stock
Salt and freshly ground black pepper

For the garlic scallops
1 clove garlic, crushed
⅛ teaspoon hot red chile flakes
2 tablespoons chopped fresh cilantro leaves
8 fresh, juicy, large scallops, roe removed
2 tablespoons olive oil

Method

1. Make the soup: Heat the oil in a pan over medium heat, add the onion, garlic, and ginger, and cook for 3 to 4 minutes, until softened. Add the cumin and coriander. Cook for 2 minutes more. Add the bell pepper, tomatoes, and the harissa. Cook over medium-low heat until the vegetables soften.

2. Add the lentils and stock and bring to a boil; reduce the heat and simmer until all the ingredients are tender, 30 to 40 minutes. Transfer to a blender and blitz to a smooth puree; season with salt and pepper to taste.

3. Make the garlic scallops: Mix the garlic, chile flakes, and half of the cilantro in a bowl, add the scallops, toss together thoroughly and marinate for 1 hour.

4. Reheat the soup.

5. Heat the oil in a frying pan over high heat until it's smoking, add the scallops, and cook for 1 minute on each side, or until golden and crusty on the exterior. Remove from the pan.

6. Pour the soup into 4 shallow serving bowls. Top each serving with 2 scallops, scatter the remaining cilantro over the soup, and serve.

seeds and nuts

All nuts and seeds indicate potential future growth, and come packed with many essential nutrients. They are high in protein (and also calories) and contain valuable oils and fat-soluble vitamins. In Southeast Asia, India, Africa, and the Middle East, nuts and seeds are combined with grains, breads, and cereals to produce an amazing assortment of high-protein dishes. And imagine Italy without pesto, the United States without peanut butter, Austria without poppy seeds.

Whenever possible, buy nuts and seeds whole, in their shells: Removing the shell at the time of use ensures maximum texture and flavor. The nutty flavor of some seeds and nuts, such as sesame seeds or pine nuts, improves if they are fried or dry-toasted. Store them in a cool, dark, dry place in order to prevent their fats from turning rancid and bitter.

1 Pumpkin seeds Inedible pumpkin kernels contain tender seeds. Often toasted with oil and salt as a snack, these are also delicious added to salads, pasta, or noodles. Include them with a mix of grains in risotto, or use them with mashed beans or peas for spicy fritters or beancakes.

2 Sunflower seeds The seeds of the glorious sunflower, when dried and shelled, have a pleasant creamy texture and taste. They can be used raw in salads, scattered into noodles, or sizzled in virgin oil and poured over rice dishes.

3 Sesame seeds These tiny, oil-rich seeds are popular in Asian cooking as a coating or garnish, and in Europe as a topping for cookies and breads. White sesame seeds (a) are immensely important and underpin many recipes, while black sesame seeds (b) have a slightly stronger, nutty, earthy flavor and are more of a curiosity. In the Indian subcontinent, they are often

tempered in hot oil and poured over grains or legumes before serving.

4 Poppy seeds Derived from the opium poppy, but not an opiate, black poppy seeds (a) have a nutty-sweet taste. Popular in Europe as a garnish, topping, or filling, they often taste best if dry-toasted. Use them on white bread, to coat white fish-balls, or in cakes and pastries. Rarer white poppy seeds (b), used in Asia and the Middle East, are scattered over flat breads or ground and used as a thickener.

5 Walnuts In many cultures, this delicious, slightly astringent nut is prized when green (for pickling), but is more commonly eaten ripe. Plain, walnuts are superb eaten with sharp Cheddar and port. Ground up, they can be used as a thickener in Circassian chicken, or in cookies.

6 Brazil nuts These rich and oily nuts from South America, ground,

make a moist meal that works well in some cakes. Whole, they are good coated in chocolate or toffee, but are most useful chopped—to add to fudge, spice loaves, or even curries or lentil patties. Brazils can also add crunch to fresh tomato, chile, and mint salsa for fish.

7 Cashew nuts These unusual and expensive nuts grow suspended beneath a red pear-shaped fruit and are never sold in the shell. Use them, plain or salted, in spicy, soy-flavored chicken dishes and Indian stir-fries. Chopped into spicy fruit and nut mixtures to fill pastries, they provide a creamy texture.

8 Pecans Related to walnuts, but with a more streamlined shape and a sweeter taste, pecans can be used in all the ways that walnuts are. They work well salted and roasted in muffins and cookies, or on cakes, and are the key to pecan pie. They are also great in ice cream sundaes with maple syrup.

9 Pine nuts (pignoli) These dense, creamy, oil-rich nuts, with a delicate resiny flavor, are the essential Mediterranean nut. Included most famously in pesto, they are also used in Italian cookies, nougat (*torrone*), and toffees. Pine nuts also add pleasurable "bite" to rice dishes.

10 Hazelnuts (filberts, cob nuts) Usually sold shelled, without their brown skins, white, tender hazelnuts are useful in both sweet and savory recipes. Try grinding them to mix with melted dark chocolate and cream for a spread, or use them whole in muesli, cookies, and cakes. Toasted, they are delicious scattered over noodles and rice.

11 Peanuts Technically, the peanut is not a nut: its parent plant is, in fact, a legume, the nuts being the peas in the pod. Sold unshelled or shelled (pictured), plain or roasted, peanuts can be ground and turned into home-made peanut butter, or used in satay and other Indonesian dishes, as well as in African chicken stews and fish curries.

12 Pistachios Grown in Greece and the Middle East, pistachios are popular worldwide. They are best bought in their tough shells (a), which can be prized apart to reveal the pink-skinned nut (b). The skin, in turn, can be removed by blanching, to reveal the luminously yellow-green flesh (c).

Add pistachios to chocolate, fudge, halva, or Turkish delight, or try them in savory dishes, such as terrines, or scatter them over white fish, for example. They are also superb pureed in ice cream.

13 Almonds These are an ancient Mediterranean food prized for their versatility, protein content, and their white, creamy interior; Jordan almonds are the most highly regarded variety.

Almonds are crucial to Greek baklava and Italian amaretti, as well as to the English Bakewell tart. They are also used in savory dishes; often with trout, and with chicken or pork in China.

9   10   11

12a   12b   12c

For use in cooking, whole almonds (a) often have their brown skins removed, in which case they are known as blanched almonds (b). The white nut can then be sliced lengthwise (c), or cut across the width to give chopped almonds (d). Finest of all are ground almonds (e).

14 Macadamia nuts Native to Australia, the buttery-mild, waxy macadamia is among the most costly and rich of nuts. Macadamias can be used in stuffings, pushed whole into meatballs, chopped into cakes, cookies, or pastries, and added to sweet fillings or chocolate truffles. They also work beautifully in home-made dukkah spice mix (see page 13).

15 Chestnuts Lean, low in starch, and high in protein, chestnuts grow best in Spain, Italy, and France. They are sometimes available dried (a), suitable for grinding to a meal to give a protein and flavor boost to breads or cakes. But chestnuts are most easily bought whole and shelled, either vac-packed or canned (b); these can be used, chopped, in stuffing, or mixed with buttery potatoes and garlic, as a mash. Chestnuts can also be bought in the form of a puree.

13a

13b

13c

13e

13d

chopping nuts and seeds

When chopping nuts or seeds, do it by hand, using a cook's knife, in repeated motions, or a mezzaluna, in a rocking motion. Alternatively, use an electric spice grinder, but only in short bursts: too much and the nuts or seeds will be reduced to an oily paste. Leaving some chunkier pieces in the ground mixture can often improve the look, texture, and mouth feel.

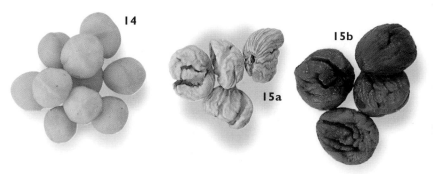

14

15a

15b

seeded bread

This bread is easy to make and has a delicious texture.

Makes 2 small loaves

Ingredients

3¾ cups all-purpose flour or bread flour
1 packet active dry instant yeast
2 tablespoons soft brown sugar
2 teaspoons sea salt flakes
3 tablespoons extra-virgin olive oil, plus more for greasing the bowl
6 tablespoons each of sesame seeds, blue poppy seeds, shelled sunflower seeds, and husked pumpkin seeds
2 tablespoons malt extract, or golden syrup
4 tablespoons honey mixed with 2 tablespoons hot water

Method

1. Put the flour, yeast, brown sugar, and salt in a bowl, and stir with a fork until they are well mixed. Add 1¼ cups warm water and just under 2 tablespoons of the oil. Mix until the dough clings together.
2. Gather the dough into a ball and tip it out onto a lightly floured work surface; knead for 2 minutes.
3. Grease a large bowl with a little oil, and put the dough in the bowl, turning it over to coat it with the oil. Cover the bowl with a plastic bag and let the dough rise, in a warm place, for 1 hour, or until it has doubled in bulk.
4. Punch the dough down. Turn it over and reshape it into a ball. Divide the ball into 2 pieces.
5. Combine the seeds, and mix them with the remaining oil and the malt extract. Pat out each ball of dough and fold the nut mixture evenly through both.
6. Shape the dough into 2 rounded loaves, put on a well-floured tray, brush with the honey mixture, and let rise in a warm place for 10 to 15 minutes. Preheat the oven to 400°F.
7. Bake for 30 to 40 minutes. Serve warm or cool, with butter.

homemade granola

This delectable recipe for an up-market version of muesli comes from the acclaimed American chef-caterer Ina Garten, known as the Barefoot Contessa. She suggests serving it with yogurt and berries, or with cold milk.

Makes 12 cups

Ingredients

4 cups old-fashioned rolled oats (not instant)
2 cups sweetened shredded coconut
2 cups sliced almonds
¾ cup vegetable oil such as grapeseed oil
½ cup good clear honey
1½ cups small-diced dried apricots
1 cup small-diced dried figs
1 cup dried cherries
1 cup dried cranberries
1 cup roasted, unsalted cashews

Method

1. Preheat the oven to 350°F.
2. Toss the oats, coconut, and almonds together in a large bowl. Whisk together the oil and honey and pour them over the oats mixture. Stir with a wooden spoon until all the oats and nuts are coated.
3. Tip the oats mixture out onto a large baking sheet (or 2 smaller ones). Bake, stirring occasionally with a spatula, until the mixture is a nice, even golden brown, about 45 minutes.
4. Remove the granola from the oven and let it cool, stirring occasionally.
5. Add the apricots, figs, cherries, cranberries, and cashews.
6. Store the cooled granola in an airtight container.

pasta, pastry, & flatbreads

pasta

Good-quality dried pasta is traditionally made using durum (hard wheat) semolina and water—look for the words "di semola di grano duro" on the label—although richer dried egg pasta ("all'uovo"), made with eggs rather than water, has grown in popularity. The best pasta is invariably Italian.

Keep a selection of pastas on hand for different uses. Long pasta is best with light, liquid sauces, whereas tubes and many of the fancy shapes now on the market are good at capturing chunky sauces. Being more absorbent, egg pasta goes well with creamy sauces, while oil-based ones are better with normal pasta. Though spinach- or tomato-flavored pastas may be authentic, most colored pastas are gimmicks and are shunned by purists, apart from good squid ink pasta, which is delicious.

Cook pasta in a large pot of boiling salted water, uncovered, until *al dente*. Drain and dress the pasta immediately, then serve. Avoid non-durum wheat or poor-quality pastas that collapse when cooked. Look for rough surfaces made using traditional bronze dies (*trafila*), indicating authentic, well-made pasta.

1 Lumaconi rigati This ridged, snail-shaped pasta tastes excellent stuffed and baked in tomato sauce, and works well in hearty recipes using meat or game sauces.

2 Macaroni (maccheroni) This tubular pasta comes in varying shapes and sizes; it is often used baked into pies, such as Greek pastitsio or macaroni and cheese, but is also good in chunky vegetable soups, or with a rich eggplant, tomato, garlic, and herb sauce.

3 Soup pasta Small pasta shapes add texture and variety to soups, especially vegetable, poultry, or meat broths. They cook quickly, so add them 10 to 15 minutes prior to the end of the soup cooking time.

4 Risi This rice-shaped pasta is often used in soups. Both risi and orzo, which is similar, only slightly larger, can be cooked in stock, as for risotto. Or try cooking either type around a lamb roast or whole roast chicken, adding chopped tomatoes, oil, and stock; the pasta absorbs the meat juices and becomes tender and crusty by the time the meat is cooked.

5 Orecchiette Literally "little ears," these small disks are excellent served with leeks, butter, Gorgonzola, and parsley, or with fresh sausage meat (ideally Italian), sautéed with cavolo nero, tomatoes, onion, and garlic. Or simply with butter, pecorino, and black pepper.

6 Penne rigate These ridged tubes are great just with butter, Parmesan, and black pepper, but also combine well with sauces such as pizzaiola (garlic, tomatoes, herbs, and black olives) and carbonara (pancetta, egg, cream, and Parmesan). Try them also with butter, garlic, onion, saffron, and mascarpone.

7 Tagliatelle Ribbonlike noodles, tagliatelle are often made from egg pasta and sold in nests, and are available in spinach (a) and other flavors, as well as plain (b). A speciality of Bologna, they are traditionally served with a meat-based ragu (Bolognese) sauce. Or use them with rich butter, cheese, or egg yolk sauces.

8 Tagliardi These thin pasta rectangles are good with light oil-, cream-, or butter-based sauces, or with thin vegetable purees, and have a lovely mouth feel. They even work well mixed with honey, brown sugar, and yogurt, as a dessert.

9 Gnocchi Italian gnocchi, usually sold vac-packed, are small dumplings made of semolina or potato. They should be poached until they float, and then dressed and served straight or baked until sizzling. Potato gnocchi go well with pesto and sizzled pine nuts. Tomato and oregano sauce suits baked semolina gnocchi, as does a wild mushroom, mascarpone, and red wine sauce.

10 Tagliolini A flat version of spaghetti (similar to linguine), tagliolini are often used in soups, but can also be used with a light dressing, such as one with olive oil, garlic, and herbs. Or use them buttered and

seasoned with rich chicken or red meat stock, and served with that same poultry or meat and herbs.

11 Pappardelle Classically served in Tuscany with game sauces, these broad egg noodles can have either straight or wavy edges. Serve them with chicken liver and sage sauce, tomato and meat ragu-type sauces, or with wild greens, sautéed with garlic, olive oil, and grated pecorino.

12 Lasagne The quick-cook sheets of pasta now available need no precooking before they are layered with meat sauce and béchamel for baked lasagne; even so, use a wet sauce for the best results. Try alternating an eggplant and roasted bell pepper layer with a béchamel and blue cheese layer, or use seafood in saffron cream sauce layered with buttered spinach.

13 Squid ink spaghetti (pasta nero) Lusciously black, glossy, and expensive, this pasta is superb eaten with olive oil, mashed anchovies, garlic, and capers; or with squid rings, scallops, garlic, cream, and tarragon. Look for pasta with a natural color additive, which is usually ink from cuttlefish rather than squid, in fact.

14 Chitarra The name refers to the guitarlike instrument used to shape

the pasta. Square in cross-section, this pasta has good "tooth feel." It is best served simply, with butter, garlic, and black pepper, or with olive oil, chiles, garlic, and parsley.

15 Bucatini Thicker than spaghetti, these long, thin tubes go well with substantial meat, vegetable, and cheese sauces; they have a firm texture, so they can also be layered in meat pies and casseroles.

16 Capellini This thread-thin pasta, also known as angel hair pasta and sometimes sold in nests, is simple and quick to cook. Use it with soupy sauces, or in actual soups. Or even add it to milky desserts, such as sweetened custards.

17 Spaghetti The best-loved pasta around the world, spaghetti excels when served simply, especially with "aglio e olio" (tossed in garlic and extra-virgin olive oil) or carbonara. It also goes very well with puttanesca sauce (tomatoes, anchovies, black olives, and capers).

18 Fusilli lunghi Twisted like a corkscrew, fusilli lunghi can take a rich eggplant, tomato, and herb sauce, or an olive and garlic paste sauce; combinations of anchovy, Parmesan, butter, or cream, garlic, and pecorino, also work well.

13   14   15   16   17   18

fusilli with arrabbiata sauce
Serves 4

Cook 18 ounces dried fusilli lunghi in boiling salted water for 12 to 14 minutes. Meanwhile, pour 4 tablespoons extra-virgin olive oil into a separate pan and add 4 chopped shallots, 2 chopped cloves garlic, and 2½ ounces canned red bell peppers (chopped). Stir in 40 black olives, 2 tablespoons dried arrabbiata mix (see page 68), 8 tablespoons tomato passata, 6 tablespoons water, and 8 chopped gherkins. When the pasta is tender, drain, then toss it in the sauce and serve sprinkled with grated Parmesan.

penne with olive, mint, and pine nut sauce
Serves 4

Cook 18 ounces penne in boiling salted water until *al dente* (9 to 12 minutes). Reserving 4 tablespoons of the cooking water, drain the pasta. Meanwhile, sauté 1 chopped onion and 2 chopped cloves garlic in 2 tablespoons extra-virgin olive oil. Push them to one side of the pan. Add ½ cup pine nuts and cook until light golden; remove the nuts and set them aside. Into the onion mixture, stir in ½ cup black olive paste or tapenade, the reserved pasta cooking water, a handful of torn fresh mint, and salt and freshly ground black pepper. Toss the drained, cooked pasta into the sauce, and stir. Serve hot, adding the pine nuts, a squeeze of lemon juice, and extra mint, if desired.

gnocchi in caper pesto
Serves 3–4

Preheat the oven to 450°F. Put 2 handfuls fresh flat-leaf parsley, 1 handful fresh mint or tarragon and 6 chopped scallions in a food processor and whiz until blended. Add 40 salted capers (rinsed and blotted dry), 4 to 6 crushed cloves garlic, 6 salted anchovies in oil (chopped), 2 tablespoons Dijon mustard, 2 tablespoons white wine vinegar and 2 tablespoons fresh lemon juice; whiz again. Cook 18 ounces potato gnocchi in boiling water, drain, and combine them with enough sauce to coat. Bake for 15 to 25 minutes, then serve plain, or with a fresh tomato salad. Any leftover sauce can be refrigerated for up to 4 days.

pappardelle with luganega sausage sauce
Serves 4

Remove the casings from 12 ounces luganega sausages (or other coarse Italian sausage). Chop and stir-fry the meat in 1 tablespoon butter, adding 1 chopped onion, 3 chopped cloves garlic, and 4 chopped fresh sage leaves. Add ½ cup white wine, then mash in 1½ tablespoons mascarpone and 1 teaspoon dried oregano. Stir, and simmer for 8 minutes. Meanwhile, cook 18 ounces dried pappardelle in boiling salted water for 6 to 8 minutes, drain, and mix with the sauce. Finally, heat 4 tablespoons extra-virgin olive oil, and add 8 chopped sage leaves; when sizzling, pour a little over each serving.

squid ink pasta with seafood sauce

This superb seafood sauce, which flatters the black squid ink spaghetti or tagliatelle outrageously well, is based on the classic Italian dish, *frutti di mare in bianco*. It is a wonderfully quick recipe: The fish is minimally cooked, and the sauce reduces while the pasta is cooking.

Serves 4

Ingredients

8 whole baby squid (about 7 ounces total), washed and drained
7 ounces salmon fillet, cut into large chunks
9 ounces monkfish, cut into large chunks
2¼ pounds fresh, live mussels, scrubbed
⅔ cup Sauvignon Blanc
1 onion, chopped
4 cloves garlic
5 tablespoons salted butter
9 ounces dried squid ink spaghetti or tagliatelle
Salt
4 tablespoons light cream
1 tablespoon potato flour
Fresh flat-leaf parsley

Method

1. Prepare the squid by cutting off the tentacle section in front of the eyes and set aside. Squeeze out any squid ink, then pull out and discard the eye area and the body contents. Remove and discard the quill.
2. Slice the body into ¾-inch rounds. Set aside with the tentacles. Pat dry the salmon and monkfish pieces.
3. Put the mussels in a heavy pan, along with the wine, onion, garlic, and half of the butter. Cover the pan and cook over medium-high heat for 4 to 5 minutes, until the mussels begin to open. Remove the mussels as they open, continuing to cook the remaining ones, covered, until all are opened. Discard any mussels that remain closed.
4. Cook the pasta in lots of boiling salted water, uncovered, for 12 to 15 minutes, until *al dente*.
5. Meanwhile, put the squid, salmon, and monkfish in the pan with the remaining butter. Cook over medium heat for 3 to 4 minutes, until the fish is firm and opaque. Remove using a slotted spoon. Set aside and keep hot, along with the cooked mussels.
6. Boil the wine mixture until reduced and flavorful. Add the cream and the butter from cooking the fish.
7. Mix the potato flour with 2 tablespoons cold water. Pour the mixture into the cream sauce. Shake and swirl the pan over high heat until the sauce is thickened. Return the cooked seafood to the sauce and reheat.
8. Serve the pasta hot with equal shares of the fish, sauce, and parsley, ideally with some chilled Sauvignon Blanc.

noodles

What most distinguishes Asian noodles from European pasta is the diversity of the starches from which they are made. Some are sold, ready-to-eat, in vac-packs, but dried noodles have a long shelf life and take only minutes to prepare: Many need only brief cooking or short immersion in hand-hot or near-boiling water. Cooking instructions on the packet can be useful, but use your own judgment: Texture and mouth feel are the chief charms of good noodles.

1 Udon These thick Japanese wheat noodles should be cooked in boiling water for 1 to 2 minutes (or 10 to 12 for dried noodles) until soft but chewy, and then rinsed. Often eaten in bowls of dashi or miso broth, udon noodles can also be eaten in less traditional fashion, with chicken, hoisin, light soy sauce, and herbs, for example.

2 Soba These buckwheat and wheat flour noodles from Japan are delicate, nutty, and delicious. Cook them in boiling water for 5 minutes, until just tender, and rinse. Serve them with miso or dashi stock, hot or spicy accompaniments, and Asian condiments.

3 Somen Thin Japanese wheat noodles, somen should have a firm, chewy texture and are normally served chilled. After cooking in boiling water (2 to 3 minutes), rinse, let cool and serve them with chilled broth, or try them with shredded nori, wasabi, and radishes.

4 Mung bean noodles Made from mung bean flour, and sometimes called cellophane or glass noodles, these are fine but tough. Put them into a bowl, cover with near-boiling water, and watch them turn opaque in a few minutes. Serve them with hot broth and other accompaniments, or in a stir-fry. They are also good in wraps and spring rolls.

5 Thai rice noodles Sold in handy bundles, these hair-thin rice noodles need to be rehydrated in hand-hot water or briefly cooked in hot stock until softened and opaque.

They can also be deep-fried. Add them to laksa soups or clear broths, or stir-fry them with shrimp, sweet-sour sauces, or fish sauce, mint, chile, ginger, and garlic.

6 Rice vermicelli Fine Chinese rice vermicelli should be soaked—in hand-hot water for 5 minutes or in cold water for 20 minutes—until pliable and opaque. Use them in cooked dishes, dressed in hot, spicy sauces and with textural additions, such as leafy vegetables, salted peanuts, Szechuan peppercorns, or fresh ginger.

7 Rice-flour noodles Made from rice flour, these Thai or Vietnamese noodles can be rehydrated in boiling water for 1 or 2 minutes (too long and they'll flop). Medium rice-flour noodles (a) are very thin, and wide noodles (b) are about ¼ inch wide. They can be served with sauces or in broths (try them in Thai green curry broth with shrimp, crunchy vegetables, and greens), or reheated in stir-fries.

8 Chinese wheat noodles These yellowish noodles need brief rehydration or cooking in hot liquids for 3 to 10 minutes (the time can vary hugely). Try them with black or yellow bean sauce, tofu, bean sprouts, and crunchy toppings.

9 Dried egg noodles These Chinese noodles, made from wheat flour and egg, come in many thicknesses and are often folded into sheets. Cook them by adding to light broths for about 5 minutes; serve in a broth, with additions such as lap cheung (see page 79); they can also be used in pad thai.

1

2

3

4

5

6 7a 7b 8 9

szechuan shrimp chow mein

This noodle recipe, by the renowned Southeast Asian food authority Sri Owen, maximizes flavors, colors, and textures, and is also extremely easy to make. "I have been asked many times why I have never put a chow mein recipe in any of my books. Chow mein simply means 'fried noodles,' so evidently the time has come to produce this recipe, which otherwise I would simply have called 'Szechuan shrimp fried noodles.'"

Serves 4

Ingredients
24 jumbo shrimp, shelled, cut in half lengthwise, and deveined
Salt
½ cup peanut oil
4 shallots, finely chopped
2 teaspoons peeled, minced ginger
1 teaspoon sugar
2 cloves garlic, very thinly sliced
4 scallions, cut into thin rounds
1 teaspoon Szechuan peppercorns, finely crushed, or 1 teaspoon chile powder
1 tablespoon Chinese rice wine or dry sherry
1 tablespoon soy sauce
3 tomatoes, peeled and chopped
½ teaspoon freshly ground black pepper
8 to 12 ounces egg noodles, cooked, refreshed under cold water, and drained
2 tablespoons chopped fresh cilantro

Method
1. Rub the halved shrimp with ½ teaspoon salt and set them aside in the refrigerator.
2. Heat 2 tablespoons of the oil in a wok over high heat. Add the shallots and ginger and stir-fry for 2 minutes. Add the sugar and garlic, and stir-fry for 1 minute. Add the scallions, peppercorns, rice wine, soy sauce, tomatoes, and pepper, and season with salt to taste. Continue stir-frying for 2 minutes.
3. In a frying pan, heat the remaining oil and, when hot, add the shrimp, stirring constantly for about 2 minutes, until just cooked. Remove them with a skimmer and transfer them to a tray lined with paper towels.
4. Put the noodles into a conical sieve and pour boiling water over them for 5 to 10 seconds, and drain well. Stir the noodles into the contents of the wok and mix well. Add the shrimp and cilantro and stir-fry for 1 minute longer. Serve immediately.

pastry doughs and wrappers

The world of pastry is one of high artistry, but it is open to anyone if they buy ready-made pastry doughs and wrappers. Both European and Asian pastry doughs are essentially vehicles, enclosing, wrapping, or providing layers for other foods. European pastry is often baked in the oven (ideally, in a convection oven on a heavy, dark metal tray, which conducts heat well) or deep-fried. Thin, fine Asian wrappers, on the other hand, can be poached, steamed, fried, or braised.

Although many fresh pastry doughs and wrappers are perishable when opened, many are now so effectively packaged that they last in any cool, dark place for at least several days, and sometimes much longer. Pastries also freeze well: Thaw them briefly before they are needed (unused wrappers can be refrozen safely).

1 Pâte sucrée This is basically shortcrust pastry that has been enriched with egg yolks, extra butter, and sugar. It is sold for use in French-style desserts, tartlets, and small sweet (and even some savory) pastries. Roll it out, chilled, on a floured surface, and try it in tarte aux poires or individual banoffee tarts.

2 Filo dough This Greek flour-and-water pastry is stretched until it is so thin that you can read print through it. It is sold in rectangular sheets, usually rolled and frozen, and can be kept pliable while in use by being covered with heavy-duty plastic wrap and a damp cloth. Brushed with melted butter or olive oil, and rolled or wrapped around fillings, it cooks in crunchy golden layers. Filo suits Greek, Turkish, and Middle Eastern sweet and savory fillings. Use it for Greek tyropitas (cheese triangles) or galacto-boureko (vanilla cream pie), for example. It can also be substituted for other similar pastries, such as *brique, yufka, ouarka,* and *malsouka.*

3 Puff pastry Most of the fat in this pastry is not in the dough mixture itself but is spread on the rolled-out dough before it is folded into its many and character-istic layers to be baked at a high temperature: The result is a light and crisp pastry, puffed up to many times its original volume. While it is possible to make puff pastry at home, it is much easier to buy the bought version, either already rolled (a) or as a block (b), which tastes good and is superbly quick. Use puff pastry with sweet or savory fillings: for Middle Eastern triangular meat, nut, or spice pastries, for example, or pithiviers (a French tart filled with a sweet almondy filling).

4 Shortcrust pastry Though easy to make at home, buying ready-made rolls (a) or blocks (b) of shortcrust pastry can save time and effort. This simple pastry is made from flour, fats (butter and/or lard), and water; if chilled, it is easy to shape. Use it for single- or double-crust pies and tarts, which are often brushed with egg before cooking. For quiches, the crust is best baked blind first, and then rebaked with the filling. Shortcrust pastry can also be used for Latin American empanadas, for frying or baking.

5 Rice paper wrappers Called *bahn trang* in Vietnamese, these wrappers come in quarter-circles or disks. They must be softened before being filled: Brush both sides with warm water or dip them briefly in water. Add 1 to 2 tablespoons crunchy Vietnamese-style stuffing, roll the wrapper up tight, and then eat with no further cooking. Serve with a Vietnamese-style salad and good dipping sauces, such as sweet chile and soy sauce.

6 Kataifi pastry This intriguing wheat pastry is most commonly used in Greek or Turkish sticky pastries. The flexible shreds can be rolled or wrapped around a food, or made into nests and filled with dried fruit or nuts, before being drizzled with melted butter or ghee and then baked; syrups are often poured over before serving. Or fill the pastry with chicken, fish, lamb, or shrimp, bake and drizzle with a sweet-sour dressing.

7 Peking duck wrappers These fine rice-flour wrappers, or pancakes, should be brushed with sesame oil and layered in a steamer or foil-lined colander to be warmed before being served with lacquered duck shreds and green herbs, hoisin and chile sauces, and salad. Or substitute crab or ham shreds. Have Asian sauces nearby for dipping.

8 Wonton wrappers Silky wonton wrappers or skins (made of wheat flour) are usually square, but can be trimmed easily, with scissors, to round. Filled and folded into various shapes, as dumplings, they suit deep-frying, though they can also be steamed or boiled in a broth. Wonton skins can also be used to make spring rolls. Or use two wrappers with a filling for a non-traditional ravioli-style dish.

9 Strudel pastry This paper-thin, stretchy, wheat-flour pastry, a more supple version of filo pastry, is sold in sheets or rolls. It should be brushed with butter, filled and then baked. Good strudel fillings include apples, spices, and crumbs, cherries with cinnamon, and sweet seed and nut fillings. Superb strudels are made in Germany, Austria, Hungary, and other central European countries.

10 Chinese dumpling wrappers These creamy-white wrappers (also called gyozo wrappers) are thicker than wonton wrappers, and are best braised or steamed. Fill them with a sesame chicken stuffing; with minced pork, ginger, garlic, cream, fermented black beans, and parsley; or with dried and fresh shrimp minced together with cilantro, scallions, carrot, and aromatics. Serve with dipping sauces and tea.

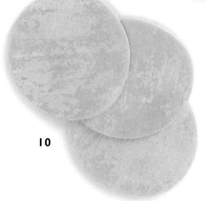

kadaifi fruit-nut pastries

Serves 4–8

Twist 8 handfuls kadaifi pastry into 8 neat nests. Set on an oiled baking sheet and bake for 40 minutes at 400°F, or until crisp. Mix 4 tablespoons scented simple syrup (see page 44) or clear honey with 8 tablespoons melted ghee or butter. Spoon some over each nest. Combine 6 prunes, about 3 tablespoons each diced dried apricots, dried cherries, dried cranberries, and mixed nuts, and 1/2 cup plus 1 tablespoon diced marzipan, and 4 tablespoons pomegranate molasses together in a food processor. Pulse until roughly chopped. Pile some on each kadaifi nest. Increase the oven temperature to 425°F and bake until golden, 15 to 20 minutes. Serve drizzled with honey mixed with fresh lemon juice.

chorizo puff pastry bracelets

Makes about 20

Roll out 14 ounces puff pastry dough to a thickness of 1/8 inch. Spread one side of the dough with 3 tablespoons harissa paste mixed with 3 tablespoons tomato paste. Scissor-chop 1 3/4 ounces sliced chorizo and sprinkle it over the paste. Fold the uncovered half of the dough over the covered surface. Press it closed and roll again. Slice the filled pastry into 1/2-inch strips and twist the ends to form "bracelets." Bake at 400°F for 18 to 20 minutes, until crisp. Serve hot, with chilled fino or amontillado sherry.

bahn trang wraps with peanuts and spicy dip
Serves 4

Assemble 8 large rice paper wrappers (*bahn trang*) and a selection of fillings, such as boiled lap cheung sausages, bamboo shoots, straw mushrooms, scallions, parsley or cilantro, yellow miso, and carrot shreds. Soften each wrapper in warm water for 30 to 40 seconds, then drain. Enclose a portion of filling in each wrapper. Wrap each in plastic wrap and chill until required. Slice diagonally in half, unwrap, and serve on mung bean noodles with a choice of moist and dry dipping accompaniments.

steamed and fried wontons
Makes 24

Have ready 32 square wonton wrappers. Make a filling by food-processing together, briefly: $3\frac{1}{2}$ ounces minced pork, lamb, or chicken; 2 teaspoons dark sesame oil; 1 (2-inch) piece peeled ginger (grated); 2 mashed cloves garlic; 4 spinach leaves; $1\frac{3}{4}$ ounces tofu; and 2 tablespoons bacon fat or heavy cream. Divide the filling into 32 balls. Center 16 of these on 16 of the wrappers. Fold two points together, making a triangle, and dampen the two narrow corners with water. With the base of the triangle facing you, bring each of the corners across two-thirds of the base line and seal. Steam for 4 to 6 minutes, until firm. With the rest of the filling, set 2 balls in the center of each of 8 dampened wrappers; press another wrapper neatly on top. Deep-fry these in oil until crisp. Serve with a dipping sauce.

flatbreads

The first flatbreads were probably made by spreading flour batters or doughs over fire-heated stones until they dried and crisped. Some are still made this way today. Many of these breads are useful in all sorts of ways, not only as snacks in their own right. They can be steam-dampened or wetted and used as wrappers; they can be pulled apart into pieces and stuffed or layered to create more complex dishes; or slit and filled with savory or sweet fillings. If sautéed or shallow fried in oil, lard, butter, or ghee, many become luxurious. Others are good oven-crisped, to be used, hot, as a vehicle for softer foods.

1 Lavash This pliable, nutty-sweet Middle Eastern bread is sold in large, thin sheets that are usually folded into squares. Dampened and reheated briefly, lavash can be eaten with hummus or babaganoush; with dukkah and olive oil; with kukuye (omelet), or spicy lamb kebabs. Filled with cheese and retoasted, it makes a good sandwich.

2 Buckwheat galettes (galettes de sarrasin) Originally from Brittany, these brownish pancakes are traditionally made of sourish and nutty buckwheat flour. Dampen and reheat them briefly in a frying pan, add ham and an egg, and then refold: delicious. Or try them, more unusually, with butter, cooked apples, and Calvados.

3 Tortillas Much imitated around the world, these Mexican flatbreads are authentically made from masa harina (see page 136), although wheat flour tortillas also exist. Good tortillas are soft, supple, and fragrant when briefly warmed, and can be used to mop up mashed refried beans, guacamole, or spicy chicken, beef, or pork; or can be stuffed and rolled as enchiladas.

4 Chapati (roti) These unleavened breads, eaten all over India and Pakistan, are made from whole wheat flour, and should be tender and speckled. Reheat them briefly, and tear off pieces to dip into soups or to scoop up curries and other hot Indian dishes.

5 Naan (nan) Many types of *naan* are made throughout Asia, but in the West it refers to the north Indian leavened bread served in any Indian restaurant. This is a puffy, soft bread, usually made of wheat flour, leavening, milk or yogurt, and seasonings. Traditionally cooked in a clay tandoor, *naan* has a characteristic smoky taste. Eat it with dhals, curries, coconut rice, and spicy chickpea dishes.

6 Pappadams These crisp Indian wafers can be bought as uncooked sheets (pictured). Cook them in hot oil, or grill or even microwave them, until puffed up and crisp. In the West, they are eaten with chutneys and relishes as an appetizer; in India they are eaten at the end of a meal.

7 Pita bread Flattish and round or oval, pitas are the most widely available breads in the eastern Mediterranean, and are integral to central and west Asian meals. Available as either plain (white) or whole wheat, warm pita can be slit open to create pockets and are perfect for foods such as falafel and salad with tahini sauce or Greek pork souvlaki.

8 Waffles (gaufres) These honeycomb-textured batter cakes, cooked in waffle irons, traditionally come from Holland, Belgium, France, and the United States. Store-bought waffles are best toasted or quick-baked and eaten with jam, ice cream, maple syrup, or simply butter or, with bacon, eggs, and syrup.

9 Pumpernickel (Schwartzbrot) This famous, whole grain rye bread from Westphalia in Germany is leavened by a sourdough culture; its dark color is a result of the caramelization of the rye during baking. Often sold sliced in rectangular blocks, it is superb as the base for open sandwiches. Eat it with cheeses, smoked sausage, or Black Forest ham and berry preserves.

10 Pikelets These traditional British yeast-leavened pancakes, griddle-cooked and with holes patterning the upper surface, are delicious eaten warm with berry jam and clotted cream, or with cream cheese and currant jelly. Drop scones and Scottish pancakes are similar.

11 Irish potato farls Mashed potatoes and flour combined in the proportion of 4:1 make a delicious damp bread, traditionally cooked as cakes, or farls, on a flat griddle. Serve the cakes toasted and buttered with soft or hard cheeses, smoked fish in cream, or sausages.

1

2

7

8

9

10

11

12

13

12 Blini These small Russian buckwheat, yeasted pancakes are traditionally served warm with caviar or cured fish, often with sour cream or melted butter. They are also excellent mashed with taramasalata.

13 Carta da mùsica These large Sardinian flatbreads, made of hard wheat flour, are delicious either brushed with olive oil and then baked or grilled until hot and crunchy, or plain, with olive, eggplant or chickpea pastes. Alternatively, soften pieces in water, to be used like softened pasta for layering in baked dishes or to wrap around a spicy filling.

5

3

4

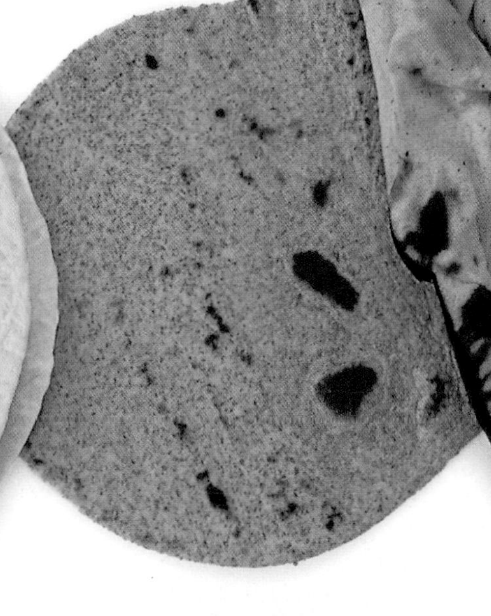

6

savory cookies

Crackers, wafers, and other savory cookies are usually crisp or crumbly ("short") in texture, flour-based, and either baked or fried. While designed for use as snacks, these cookies can be broken, crushed, or powdered for other uses, whether as a crisp topping, or as a crumb-crust base for savory cheesecakes or tartlets, or to give crunch to soft salads. They are superbly useful.

1 Bruschettini Dried, oven-crisped slices of bruschetta can be crushed finely as a gratin topping for sliced eggplant or lasagne, or coarsely crushed for use in meatballs. They can also be dampened with olive oil and used as the basis of Italy's famous panzanella salad.

2 Matzo crackers Made of flour and water, this unleavened Jewish bread is crisp and flaky. The crackers can be crushed and used as bread crumbs for toppings and coverings.

3 Scandinavian rye crispbreads These cookies are thick, strong, and crusty but light, low in fat, and high in fiber. Eat them with cured meats and hard cheeses, or break them up into hot milk and add honey, for a quick, unorthodox breakfast.

4 Scottish oatcakes Shaped into rounds or triangles (farls), these cookies are so brittle that Scots usually lay (rather than spread) butter on top of them. They can be crumbled over baked vegetables or into barley and vegetable soups.

5 High-baked water biscuits Dark-dappled water biscuits have a distinctive, toasty taste and a hard yet flaky texture. Crushed to fragments or a powder, they can be used, with savory spices, as part of a mixture to scatter on potato-topped cottage pies before baking.

6 Scottish rye wafers These scrumptious hexagonal wafers, sometimes dotted with seeds, are good with both sweet and savory spreads. Try using them to sandwich cream cheese and smoked salmon.

7 Saltines Perforated for easy breaking, these biscuits are found worldwide. Baked hard and dry, they were once a staple food for sailors on long voyages, and are sometimes known as ship's biscuits. Eat them with fish or corn chowder.

8 Rice cakes These spongy, low-fat, and gluten-free cookies can be utterly flavorless or delicious. The best are flavored with sesame, soy sauce, salt, or seaweed. Try crumbling them, to mix with dried fruit and nuts, like muesli, or to add extra texture to salads.

9 Shrimp toasts Flavored with shrimp or fish, these deep-fried crackers are delicious if made in Indonesia; Chinese versions are more variable in quality. Eat them with fresh, spicy relishes or sambals, or with coconut-based fish dishes.

10 Melba toasts These wheat-flour toasts do not break or soften quickly if buttered. They can be crushed and used, with cayenne and melted butter, as a crumb base for savory cheesecakes, or as a tasty coating for fish cakes.

11 Cheese wafer thins Very cheesy, these flaky Dutch cookies are much copied but rarely bettered. Coarsely crushed, they make a gratin topping. Finely crushed, they add color, texture, and savor to smoked fish pies. Or toast them briefly and crumble them over a soft cheese and watercress salad.

flours & cooking aids

flours and thickening agents

Flours can be used to make everything from bread to puddings, to thicken sauces, and to add crispness to fried foods: They are multifunctional. Although flour can be made from all sorts of starchy foods, on its own the word usually means wheat flour. Wheat (*Triticum*) is special in that it contains gluten (a stretchy protein that helps make dough light and airy). It exists in thousands of varieties—many common wheat flours are varieties of *Triticum aestivum*—all containing different amounts of gluten: High-gluten hard wheat flours are used to make bread, while low-gluten soft wheat flours are used for cakes. Thus, it is usually important to match the right flour to the recipe.

Starchy thickening agents must usually be mixed (or slaked) in a little cold water before being added to a hot liquid, to avoid the formation of lumps, or else mixed to a paste with butter.

1 White flour Highly milled white, or all-purpose, flour from soft or medium wheat grain is good for most purposes. The fine grains can absorb large quantities of liquid and sugar, which produces a softer finish perfect for cakes, doughs, sauces, and batters.

Cake flour is a specially treated all-purpose flour that is super-soft and very absorbent. Self-rising flour is all-purpose white flour with leavening agents added.

Italian doppio zero flour (00, or "double-zero," flour) is a soft white flour perfect for making pasta at home (most soft wheat flours make only passable pasta dough), particularly in combination with semolina.

2 Bread flour This flour suits bread making because it is made from a hard variety of *Triticum aestivum* that is high in gluten; additional gluten may also be added. The elasticity of the gluten is activated by kneading, and gives bread its characteristic fibrous structure when it is baked.

3 Buckwheat flour Ground buckwheat is used in Russian blini, Breton crêpes, and in breakfast pancakes. It has a fairly strong, nutty, and astringent taste, which is not to

everyone's liking. Combining it half and half with wheat flour is a good option.

4 Polenta flour This finely ground maize flour is a finer version of cornmeal or polenta (see page 107). It adds sweetness, color, and protein to cornbreads, country breads, pancakes, dessert cakes, and biscuits; it is used in Portugal's famous yeasted cornbreads.

5 Masa harina This lime-treated, precooked flour, made from ground corn, is essential in Mexican cuisine and has a distinctive taste and puttylike texture when mixed to a dough. Rolled or pressed flat, masa harina dough makes tortillas. The flour can also be used as a thickener, in baking, or to bind mixtures, or coat foods for frying.

6 Coarse-grain flour (granary) Though the name "granary" is a proprietary term, it is commonly used to describe nutty, toasty, three-wheat flour with malted grains. Use it for breads, scones, batters, malt bread, and even cakes.

7 Ground rice This sandy-textured flour, made from polished white rice, is used in many Jewish, Indian, Middle Eastern, and European dishes. As well as thickening milky puddings, soups, and stews, ground rice helps produce crispness in batters, doughs, cakes, and cookies. Try it in *keskül* (Turkish almond custard) and Scottish shortbread.

8 Gram flour Made of ground chickpeas or other dried peas or beans, this nutty flour is popular in India, and parts of Italy and France. Chickpea flour is used, famously, in socca (pancakes sold in the streets of Provence). In India, gram flour is used in fritters and savory breads. It contains next to no gluten.

9 Spelt flour This ancient form of wheat, which still thrives in the Balkans, has complex, lively flavors, and is less genetically modified than ordinary wheat flours. When used in bread dough, spelt flour rises quicker than usual, but collapses if left to rise for too long.

10 Whole wheat flour This flour is made from the whole wheat grain, including both the bran (fibrous outer layer) and the nutritious germ. (Ordinary "brown" flour has some of the bran and germ extracted.) Whole wheat flour may be made of soft or hard wheat, the latter being used to make strong whole wheat flour for bread making. Stone-ground flours, using traditional millstones rather than rollers, are the best: The flour has a better flavor and mouth feel.

11 Chestnut flour (farina di castagne) Once important in certain rural areas of France and Italy, this sweet chestnut flour is gluten-free, starchy, and protein-rich, so it adds density and richness to batters, doughs, and cakes. Try it in bitter chocolate puddings or in flattish country breads, mixed with spelt flour or strong bread flour.

12   13   14   15

16   17   18   19

20

12 Cornstarch Commonly used to thicken sauces, gravies, casseroles, and milky desserts, cornstarch, when used 1:3 with wheat flour, can also lighten cakes, batters and some cookies. Its main problem is that it can turn gelatinous and look cloudy rather than remaining clear and smooth. However, it does not break down when frozen, so is useful for stews to be stored in the freezer.

13 Arrowroot This superfine powder, from the *Maranta* plant, produces a soft, stable, crystal-clear gel, which makes great glazes for peach or apricot tarts, clear sauces for poached chicken breast, or shiny sauces for pork spareribs. Slaked in cold water and stirred into hot liquid, arrowroot cooks quickly: Remove the liquid from the heat straight away, or it may thin again.

14 Tapioca starch This fine starch made from cassava (manioc) root is often used in Asian dishes, to thicken meat mixtures, coconut or dairy milk sauces, soups, and desserts, or to help create smooth batters for pancakes and omelets. Mixed with water, it can also thicken stock or fruit-based sauces.

15 Tapioca These curious, hard grains are starch granules extracted from cassava root. Cooked in dilute liquids, they soften, swell, and gelatinize, thereby thickening the cooking liquid so that it sets. Many Scandinavian and Asian desserts, fruit soups, and drinks contain tapioca. Tapioca pearls (pictured) are larger than normal tapioca, and require soaking for several hours in cold water before use.

16 Rice starch Made from glutinous rice and much finer than ground rice, this thickener makes an elegant and crisp surface coating for foods to be steamed or fried. Use it to lighten doughs, cakes, and batters (it keeps deep-fried squid crunchy), and to thicken delicate dessert sauces.

17 Custard powder This yellow powder contains cornstarch, salt, flavoring, and annatto. As well as being used for custard (ideally with added sugar, egg yolks, and cream), it is also good for creating a stable, glossy gel for butterscotch, caramel, or mocha sauces.

18 Potato flour Also called fécule or fecula, this delicate potato starch is a useful thickener. It needs only 40 to 50 seconds' cooking time, and gives a sheer, glossy effect. It can be used, with egg and milk, to make tiny potato pancakes, and can improve the texture of potato bread and dumplings. Use it 1:2 with wheat flour for lighter cakes.

19 Purple yam flour This pretty flour, made from dried and ground yams, works well in sticky, thickened desserts, as well as in pastries, doughs, and cakes.

20 Kudzu powder A dense Japanese thickener, made from the roots of the kudzu vine, this tends to clump into odd angular shapes, which can be crushed using a pestle and mortar. It is excellent for giving gloss and body to vegetable stews, or for dredging pork, fish, or chicken strips before deep-frying, to produce a light and crisp surface.

storage

Store flour airtight, on a cool, dark, dry and airy shelf. Plain flour can keep for up to six months, but whole wheat flour is best used within two months, since the oil in the germ tends to go rancid. Buy small volumes, often.

cooking aids

While some of these intriguing items have only occasional relevance, many can greatly improve the taste, consistency, looks, or authenticity of a dish. Some, such as cochineal, are merely cosmetic; others, such as baking powder or gelatin, are structural components that utterly identify a particular recipe or improve the ease of making it.

The effectiveness of some cooking aids, particularly leavening agents, wanes over time. Always check the "best before" date, and store in a cool, dark, and dry place.

1 Glycerin This sticky syrup is useful to help retain moistness, gloss, and softness in foods such as glacéed and crystallized fruits. It is also valuable for delaying the setting of cake icings when undertaking time-consuming decoration. Only tiny amounts are needed.

2 Vegetable rennet This liquid coagulant is a vegetarian version of the more traditional rennet enzyme found in the stomachs of ruminants. It is used to set milk-based mixtures into curds and whey for the dessert called junket: About 10 drops will set 2⅓ cups of tepid milk (at 90°F). Try it for almond or vanilla and rose water junket.

3 Glucose syrup A synonym for dextrose, glucose syrup can be used to modify crystallization in

home-made "soft-scoop" ice cream, to create nougatine (a pliable form of nougat), or as edible "glue," for attaching cake decorations.

4 Cochineal An intense red liquid food coloring produced by crushing an insect found on Central American cacti can be useful for creating pink icing for cakes or red cherry pie glaze. (The nearest vegetable red pigment equivalents include beet juice or, better still, red sorrel.)

5 Baking powder Cream of tartar and bicarbonate of soda used to be the standard raising agents, but now ready-made baking powders are more common. This type requires heat as well as liquid to be activated, so any delay between mixing and baking is not disastrous.

6 Bicarbonate of soda Also known as sodium bicarbonate or baking soda, this alkaline powder, mixed with acid (such as cream of tartar or lemon juice), produces carbon dioxide to "raise" flour mixtures; it should be mixed in just before baking, since otherwise the gas dissipates. Adding bicarbonate of soda to the water when cooking beans can soften the skins and make them easier to digest.

7 Cream of tartar This mildly acidic powder, used 2:1 with an alkali such as bicarbonate of soda, creates a homemade baking powder that activates on mixing with liquid. A pinch can improve the volume and lightness when whisking egg whites for meringues, and discourage the formation of crystals in sugar syrups during cooking.

8 Ascorbic acid (vitamin C) This crystalline powder, available at drugstores, can speed up rising when using yeast in bread doughs. It also helps to preserve naturally vivid colors, such as the red pigments in strawberry jam, as well as to safeguard vitamin levels and boost flavors. Add some to home-made lemonade, or to black currant or raspberry coulis or sauces.

9 Instant yeast Also known as fast-acting or micronized yeast, this powder-fine yeast, sold in 1/4-ounce packets, is the equivalent of 1.6 ounces compressed yeast, or 1 tablespoon regular dry yeast. The huge advantage of instant yeast is that, unlike dry or compressed yeast, it is added directly to the flour, and no proofing in liquid is needed.

10 Gelatin Made from animal hides and bones, this setting agent can be used to set fruit or wine jellies, aspics, and mousses. Both granulated gelatin (a) and leaf or sheet gelatin (b) need to be softened in cold liquid before being heated over boiling water until clear (they must not boil), and then whisked into the (ideally warmed) liquid to be set. Let cool and then chill for 2 to 6 hours to set.

11 Rice paper This papery, edible base for sweets and confections is made of the pithy stems of a Chinese shrub. Use it as a surface on which to mold, pipe, or place sticky, fragile, or delicate chocolate, toffee, caramel, marshmallow, or fudge mixtures, or for macaroons.

12 Agar-agar This setting agent, made from seaweed, is popular in Asian cooking and useful for vegetarians who would rather not use animal-based gelatin. Available either as granules (a) or strands (b), agar-agar can be simply stirred into the liquid to be set, boiled briefly (agar-agar will dissolve only in boiling water), and then stirred until thickened. Let cool and leave to set. Less agar-agar than gelatin is needed to set the same volume of liquid.

13 Panko (Japanese bread crumbs) The best bought bread crumbs are these light Japanese crumbs, sold either coarse (pictured) or fine. They are used to coat sliced and egg-dipped seafood, fish or meat for frying (for Japanese furai dishes), but are so light that they can be used in cake recipes. They can also make "instant" bread sauce, with ground cloves. Sautéed in butter they are delicious on noodles, too.

13

12a

12b

10b

11

10a

sweet scones
Makes 6–8

Baking powder, as well as self-rising flour, is the secret of good scones, as is quick, minimal handling. Preheat the oven to 450°F. Mix together 2¼ cups self-rising flour, 2 teaspoons baking powder, a pinch of salt, and 5 teaspoons superfine sugar. Cut in 5 tablespoons plus 1 teaspoon cubed butter until the mixture looks like coarse bread crumbs. Whisk together 1 egg and scant ½ cup milk. Stir the milk mixture into the dry ingredients to form a soft dough. Turn the dough out and knead it lightly, using floured fingertips (not a rolling pin), to about 1 inch thick. Cut into 6 to 8 rounds. Bake for 10 to 12 minutes, or until crusty and golden. Let cool slightly on a rack. Serve warm with butter, strawberry jam, and crème fraîche or other thick cream.

cranberry tapioca and cream
Serves 4

This old-fashioned recipe is updated by the use of a microwave oven; it uses cranberry juice drink, which has a long shelf life and a great color. Mix 6 tablespoons tapioca (if you use the large pearls, these must be soaked in water for 3 to 8 hours first), rinsed, and 1¼ cups cranberry juice drink in a measuring jug. Stir well, cover with a plate, and cook in a microwave oven at high power for 20 minutes, stirring after 10 minutes. Stir in 4 to 6 tablespoons sugar and another ⅔ cup cranberry juice. Cook for 10 minutes longer, or until no hard white centers are visible in the tapioca, and it feels soft and jellylike. Stir in ½ cup extra cranberry drink, and also 1 tablespoon dark rum, brandy, or Cointreau. Pour into 4 serving glasses. Trickle light cream on top and decorate with fresh berries. Serve warm or at room temperature.

suppliers

The following list includes sources of the ingredients featured in the photographs in this book, as well as other useful suppliers and producers of fine foods.

HERBS, SPICES, AND CONDIMENTS:
The Great American Spice Company
P.O. Box 80068, Fort Wayne, IN 46898
260-420-8118
888-502-8058
www.americanspice.com
Spices and dry goods, from popular to hard-to-find. Also a full range of snacks, mixes, condiments, sauces and oils.

Kitchen/Market
218 Eighth Avenue
New York, NY 10011
212-243-4433
www.kitchenmarket.com
Kitchen/Market offers one of the largest selections of chile peppers in the United States, as well as many other fine cooking ingredients.

Kalustyans
123 Lexington Ave
New York, NY 10016
212-685-3451
www.kalustyans.com
Around since 1944, this shop has a wide variety of middle eastern and Indian herbs and spices, as well as food supplies and ingredients from all over the world.

Sira Cash & Carry
Penzeys Spices
19300 W Janacek Ct
Brookfield, WI 53045
800-741-7787
262-785-7637
Other locations around the country
www.penzeys.com
Wide variety of herbs, spices and seasonings, plus specialty spices from around the world.

Adriana's Caravan
321 Grand Central Terminal
New York, NY 10017
800-316-0820
212-972-8804
www.adrianascaravan.com

Companion Plants
7247 N. Coolville Ridge Road
Athens, Ohio 45701
740-592-4643
www.companionplants.com
Wide variety of live plants, herbs, seeds, roots and mushrooms

Well-Sweep Herb Farm
205 Mount Bethel Road
Port Murray, New Jersey 07865
908-852-5390
www.wellsweep.com
One of the largest collections of herbs and perennials in the country with over 1875 varieties, from the familiar and unusual to the rare and exotic.

Moon Shine Trading Company
1250-A Harter Ave.
Woodland, California 95776
800-678-1226
www.moonshinetrading.com
Gourmet honey and a wide range of varietals, plus honey products

FINE CHOCOLATE:
L.A. Burdick Chocolate
P.O. Box 593
Main Street
Walpole, NH 03608
800-229-2419
www.burdickchocolate.com
Handmade chocolates.

La Maison du Chocolate
1018 Madison Avenue
New York, NY 10021
212-744-7117
30 Rockefeller Center
New York, NY 10020
212-265-9404
Parisian company with two locations in New York City.

Hawaiian Vintage Chocolate
1050 Bishop Street, Suite 162
Honolulu, HI 96813
808-735-8494
www.hwvi.com
Aged chocolate organically grown on the Big Island of Hawaii.

Richart New York
7 E 55th Street
New York, NY 10022
212-371-9369

Richart San Francisco
928A Van Ness Avenue
San Francisco, CA 94109
415-351-1800

PRESERVED FRUITS, VEGETABLES, NUTS AND SEEDS:
June Taylor Jams
Available at the San Francisco Ferry Plaza Farmers' Market, by mail order, and at a variety of retailers throughout the country.
Correspondence address:
424 62nd Street
Oakland, CA 94609
510-923-1522
www.junetaylorjams.com
Organic marmalades and conserves made with handcut fruit, without additives or pectin and with a minimum of sugar.

PRESERVED MEATS, CHARCUTERIE, SAUSAGES:
Hobbs' Applewood Smoked Meats
San Rafael, CA 94901
415-453-0577
www.fbworld.com/HobbsSmkMeats.htm
Artisan cured meats, such as apple wood smoked bacon, hams, sausages, and salami. Primarily a supplier to bay area restaurants, call for minimum quantities. These meats are also available at some retailers, such as Dean & Deluca and Whole Foods.

Niman Ranch
Correspondence:
1025 East 12th Street
Oakland, CA 94606
510-808-0340

www.nimanranch.com
Beef, pork and lamb from livestock that are humanely treated, fed natural feeds (with no animal by-products or waste), never given growth hormones or sub-therapeutic antibiotics, and raised on land that is cared for as a sustainable resource. Niman Ranch is available online and at a number of grocery stores throughout the country.

FISH AND SEAFOOD:
Caviarteria
502 Park Avenue (at 59th St.)
New York, NY 10022
212-759-7410
800-4-CAVIAR
www.caviarteria.com
With locations nationwide, Caviateria offers a variety of caviars as well as smoked salmon and foie gras.

Russ and Daughters
179 E. Houston St.
New York, NY 10002
212-475-4880
800-RUSS-229 from outside the New York tri-state area.
www.russanddaughters.com
Caviar, smoked and cured salmon, other smoked fish, as well as imported cheeses and sweets, since 1914.

OILS AND VINEGARS:
California Olive Oil Corporation
134 Canal Street
Salem, Massachusetts 01970
978-745-7840
www.olive-oil.com
A variety of oils and vinegars, gourmet, organic and infused. Since 1945, the country's oldest purveyor of fine oils, vinegars and gourmet products.

St. Helena Olive Oil Company
P.O. Box 389
8576 St. Helena Hwy
Rutherford, CA 94573
800-939-9880
www.sholiveoil.com
Napa Valley gourmet olive oils and vinegars.

O Olive Oil
1854 Fourth Street
San Rafael, CA 94901
888-827-7148
www.oolive.com
California citrus olive oils, imported oils, vinegars.

CHEESES AND DAIRY:
Tomales Bay Foods
80 Fourth Street
Point Reyes Station, CA 94956
415-663-9335
www.tomalesbayfoods.com
Artisan cheeses.

Project Truffle
460 Fair Oaks St.
San Francisco, CA 94110
866-328-7325
www.projecttruffle.com
Online partner of Tomales Bay Foods and source for artisan cheeses.

Ideal Cheese Shop Ltd.
942 1st Ave
New York, NY 10022
800-382-0109
www.idealcheese.com

Murray's Cheese Shop
257 Bleecker Street
New York, NY 10014
888-692-4339
www.murrayscheese.com

Fox & Obel
401 East Illinois
Chicago, IL 60611
312-410-7301
www.fox-obel.com
Fox and Obel has more than 300 varieties of cheese, including an unsurpassed offering of artisanal cheeses from around the globe. This gourmet market also offers a full range of foods, from exotic to everyday.

The Cheese Store of Beverly Hills
419 N. Beverly Drive
Beverly Hills, CA 90210
310-278-2855
800-547-1515
www.cheesestorebh.com
Hundreds of hard to find cheeses, as well as oils, vinegars, truffles, meats, foie gras, and caviar.

Central Market
3815 Westheimer
Houston, TX 77027
713-386-1700
Over 700 cheeses from around the world.

DELIS AND ETHNIC GROCERS:
Paulina Meat Market
3501 North Lincoln
Chicago, IL 60657
773-248-6272
Old-world meat market and homemade sausages.

Citarella
2135 Broadway
New York, NY 10023
212-874-0383
Other locations:
1313 Third Avenue
1250 Avenue of the Americas
424 Avenue of the Americas
www.citarella.com

Ready Meats
3550 Johnson Street NE
Minneapolis, MN 55418
612-789-2484
www.readymeats.com
Since 1946, Ready Meats offers a full range of meats, plus Swedish (and Italian) specialties.

Wasserman and Lemberger
7006-D Reisterstown Road
Baltimore, MD 21215
410-486-4191
Kosher butcher and delicatessen.

Katz's Delicatessen
205 E. Houston
New York, NY 10002
www.homedelivery.com/katz.htm
Jewish style deli with a full range of deli meats, Knishes, and cheesecakes.

Eli's Vinegar Factory
431 East 91st Street
New York, NY 10128
www.elizabar.com/vinegar.html
Gourmet market with greenhouses on the roof.

Zabar's
2245 Broadway (at 80th St.)
New York, NY 10024
800-697-6301
www.zabars.com
Gourmet market offering an enormous range of foods and housewares.

Dean and Deluca
560 Broadway
New York, NY 10012
212-226-6800
www.deandeluca.com
Three other locations in New York City, as well as locations in St. Helena, CA, Leawood, KS, Charlotte, NC, and Washington, DC

Whole Foods
www.wholefoods.com
Natural and organic products, now with 143 locations nationwide.

Salumeria Italiana
151 Richmond St
Boston, MA 02109
617-523-8743
800-400-5916
www.salumeriaitaliana.com
Italian market in Boston's North End, as well as an online shop.

A. Esposito
1001 S. 9th Street
Philadelphia, PA 19147
215-922-2659
www.phillyitalianmarket.com

Part of the Philadelphia 9th Street Italian Market, this butcher and Italian market has been there since 1911.

Molinari Delicatessen
373 Columbus Avenue
San Francisco, CA 94133
www.lifestylesaz.com/ads/molinari/default.asp
Italian market offering deli meats, cheeses, pasta, and other Italian delicacies

DiPalo Fine Foods
206 Grand Street
New York, NY 10013
212-226-1033
High quality Italian specialty foods.

Epicure Market
1656 Alton Road
Miami Beach, FL 33139
305-673-3488
www.epicuremarket.com

Gourmet Garage
2567 Broadway
New York, NY 10025
212-941-1664
Other locations:
453 Broome Street
301 East 64th Street
117 7th Avenue South
www.gourmetgarage.com

Cardullo's Gourmet Shoppe
6 Brattle Street
Cambridge, MA 02138
617-491-8888
800-491-8288
www.cardullos.com
Specialty foods and beverages, from honeys and chocolates, wines and beers, teas and coffees, to British and French specialties and cheeses.

Kam Man Food Products
200 Canal St.
New York, NY 10013
212-571-0330
Chinese grocery Kam Man specializes in fresh and bulk foods, including barbecued meats, fresh water chestnuts, fresh and dried fish, pickled vegetables, dozens of soy and hoisin sauces, a broad selection of fresh vegetables, and specialties from Vietnam and Thailand.

CANADIAN SUPPLIERS

Ambika Enterprises Inc
5125 Victoria Drive
Vancouver, B.C. V5P 3V1
(604) 327-0295
Herbs and spices

The Cookbook Company
722-11th Avenue SW
Calgary, AB T2R 0E4
(403) 265-6066
Gourmet speciality foods and hard-to-find ingredients

The Gourmet Warehouse
1856 Pandora Street
Vancouver, B.C. V5L 1M5
(604) 253-3022
Wide range of gourmet ingredients

Lina's Italian Market
2202 Centre Street NE.
Calgary, AB T2E 2T5
(403) 277-9166
Quality Italian produce

Phoenix Ranch Market
5833 S. Central Ave.
Phoenix, AZ 85040
602-276-3800
Authentic Mexican market.

Savenor's Supermarket
160 Charles Street
Boston, MA 02114
617-723-6328
A gourmet market with a selection of exotic meats, from buffalo to rattlesnake.

Loblaws
www.loblaws.ca
Wide range of produce. A selection of speciality departments and shops on one site.

Overwaitea Food Group
www.owfg.com
Wide range of produce. Western Canada's leading food retailer.

Parthenon
3080 West Broadway
Vancouver, B.C. V5P 3V1
(604) 733-4191
Excellent selection of homemade and packaged Mediterranean foods

Safeway
www.safeway.com
All foods. Includes 21 Carrs stores in Alaska.

Sobeys
www.sobeys.ca
Wide range of produce

bibliography

Alexander, Stephanie, *The Cook's Companion* (Viking, 1996).

Bayless, Rick and Deann Groen, *Authentic Mexican – Regional Cooking from the Heart of Mexico* (William Morrow & Company, 1987)

Beer, Maggie. *Maggie's Table* (Viking, 2001)

Bharadwaj, Monisha, *The Indian Pantry* (Kyle Cathie, 1996)

Blanc, Raymond, *Foolproof French Cookery* (BBC Books, 2002)

Garten, Ina, *Barefoot Contessa Parties!* (Clarkson Potter Publisher, 2001)

Gayler, Paul, *Flavours of the World* (Kyle Cathie, 2002)

Owen, Sri, *Noodles the New Way* (Quadrille, 2000)

Puck, Wolfgang, *Pizza, Pasta and More* (Random House, 2000)

Roden, Claudia, *The Book of Jewish Food* (Knopf, 1997)

Roux, Michel, *Sauces* (Quadrille, 1996)

Salaman, Rena, *Greek Food* (Harper Collins, 1993)

Stein, Rick, *Rick Stein's Food Heroes* (BBC Books, 2002)

Vongerichten, Jean-Georges, and Mark Bittman, *Cooking at Home with a Four-Star Chef* (Broadway Books, 1998)

Wolfert, Paula, *The Cooking of South West France* (Grub Street, 1999)

acknowledgements

AUTHOR: This book has been a huge undertaking, and teamwork was essential. My heartfelt thanks to the following friends, colleagues, researchers, and assistants, without whom this book would still be languishing in the drawer: Vicki Peterson, for research, tasting, and word processing; Janine Ratcliffe, Bob Larkins, and Barrabel Mason for research, testing, and tasting; Pippa Cuthbert for research, testing, tasting, and word processing; Emma Robertson for testing and tasting; also Janine Ratcliffe and Emma McIntosh for food styling assistance. Many thanks also to Emily Hatchwell, Janet James, Madeline Weston, David Munns, and Victoria Allen for their support above and beyond the call of duty.

PUBLISHER: We would like to thank the following for contributing recipes to this book (in order of appearance): Rick and Deann Groen Bayless, Jean-Georges Vongerichten, Rena Salaman, Maggie Beer, Raymond Blanc, Michel Roux, Claudia Roden, Paul Gayler, Rick Stein, Paula Wolfert, Wolfgang Puck, Stephanie Alexander, Monisha Bharadwaj, Ina Garten, and Sri Owen.

All guest recipes are used with permission.

index